"This book saves people from sui___ ___ loneliness. When I read this book, I can't help but cry. But these are not ordinary tears. These are tears of happiness that Christ will never forsake me."

Letter from an abused woman

"The book carried me along and turned out to be so gripping that I 'swallowed,' I mean devoured the whole of it at one go. I find it hard to explain in English. It has made an atheist read the Bible in a completely different way – not just as a literary relic but as something much more profound and meaningful. The story is so astonishingly frank and open-hearted, and touching, and horrible, and encouraging at the same time. I just cannot imagine how she ... survived."

Atheist student from Moscow

"Your book shocked me. It's written with emotional language people understand. There are answers to many painful questions: Why do I have to suffer so much? Why can't I be happy? I think your understanding of God's Word and its incarnation in your life helps many people believe in God and not to grumble at the suffering, which He sends us."

Another university student

"God evidently entrusts some of His choice servants with gut-wrenching suffering so that the whole body will be strengthened. Valetta's willingness to be transparent and vulnerable enables us to see her tenacious hope in a trustworthy God. We see radiance through tears and light in the darkness. Her faith through what could have been totally devastating experiences makes the reality of a personal relationship with a personal God clear. This book is deep, heart and personal, a must for all who are walking a journey of heartbreak and suffering."

Bette Crouse
Retired One Mission Society Missionary to Korea and
CoMission Trainer

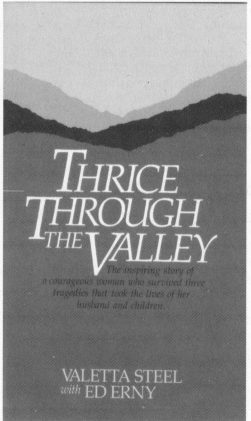

THRICE THROUGH THE VALLEY

The inspiring story of
a courageous woman who survived three
tragedies that took the lives of her
husband and children.

VALETTA STEEL
with ED ERNY

Original Version of *Another Valley, Another Victory*

Another
VALLEY

Another
VICTORY

OMS · ONE MISSION SOCIETY

By God's grace, One Mission Society unites, inspires, and equips Christians to make disciples of Jesus Christ, multiplying dynamic communities of believers around the world.

One Mission Society is an evangelical, interdenominational faith mission that makes disciples of Jesus Christ through intentional evangelism, planting churches, forming strategic partnerships, and training national leaders in Africa, Asia, the Caribbean, Europe, Latin America, and the Middle East. One Mission Society then joins with those churches in global partnerships to reach the rest of the world.

One Mission Society
PO Box A
Greenwood, IN 46142
317.888.3333

www.onemissionsociety.org
http://oms.media

Another
VALLEY

Another
VICTORY

Three Tragedies,
One Faithful Woman,
Victory in Jesus

Valetta Steel Crumley

With Ed Erny

OMS · ONE MISSION SOCIETY

Printed in the United States of America

One Mission Society

P.O. Box A

Greenwood, Indiana 46142

317.888.3333

www.onemissionsociety.org

http://oms.media

Paperback ISBN: 978-1-62245-308-5

eBook ISBN: 978-1-62245-309-2

10 9 8 7 6 5 4 3

Available where books are sold.

CONTENTS

I've tried many times to analyze the phenomenon of tragedy – how a single moment, a single event, a single word can forever alter the shape of one's world. The mind struggles to comprehend, yet it revolts. The heart will not accept what reason insists is fact. Then, slowly, at intervals, the facts begin to seep down from the numbed brain into the heart, bringing a kind of paralysis. At the same time comes a vague, nagging sense of guilt. *Why me? Why us?* are the questions that intrude, again and again. *Where did we fail? Was there something we could have done that we didn't do? Is God punishing us?*

—Valetta Crumley

1

THE VALLEY'S APPROACH

Looking back on that day, I struggle to remember just how it was.

It began as any other winter day, the smoky February sun gradually illuminating, but hardly warming, the lifeless landscape. As I sat down to the breakfast table, out of the corner of my eye I watched Lorna, my fifteen-year-old daughter, impatiently pulling a comb through her long blonde tresses.

She threw a maroon coat over her small shoulders. "Bye, Mom," she shouted and hurried out the door in pursuit of the school bus. It was Friday.

Midmorning and still nothing to distinguish this day from a hundred others. At my desk in the mission's office where I worked, I wrestled with the news release that would be due on Monday morning.

The phone rang. It was Leon, my seventeen-year-old son, who was happily working through his freshman year of college at Greenville, Illinois.

"Mom," he began excitedly, "can you pick me up this afternoon? Our concert has been scratched. It would be great if I could come home."

"Sure, Leon," I answered. His deep maturing voice sent a warm glow through me. Now that he was older, bursting with ideas and dreams, talkative and challenging, taking his father's place as the man of the family, there was a rich and growing bond between us.

"It'd be great to have you home for the weekend. What time should I come?"

Three weeks earlier, Leon had jammed clothing and an accumulation of his most prized belongings into a couple of suitcases and headed for Greenville, a church school on the flat, featureless plains of southern Illinois.

Still seventeen, he had finished high school at midyear, graduating with honors. Through the summer, he had seemed like a thoroughbred at the starting gate, impatiently pawing the track. "College will be super," he confided. "I just know it."

His first call home brought news that he had been asked to join a campus musical group.

"They're called *The Re-Created*," he explained. "Neat kids. It's really an honor to be invited. We'll be out weekends sharing Christ."

I left my office at noon. Sliding behind the wheel of my blue Montego, I eased out into the traffic flowing along US 31 toward the heart of Indianapolis, past the suburban landmarks familiar to a thousand communities – a local shopping mall, Sears, Ponderosa, Burger King.

Off the beltline, I soon was on Interstate 70, heading west. The highway stretched before me like a broad gray divider, intersecting acres of corn fields and a succession of small Indiana towns that magically stir to life every Friday night when Indiana basketball fever takes over.

It was midafternoon and getting colder when I pulled off the interstate into the sleepy village of Greenville, its substantial brick homes and well-ordered streets inevitably leading to the campus of Greenville College.

Turning into the parking lot, I switched off the ignition and paused, wondering where to begin my search for Leon. Then, before I could open the door, Leon appeared as if from nowhere. As I looked up at his six-foot frame, I felt a surge of pride. The wide smile showed a row of evenly spaced white teeth. Gentle blue eyes. I noted a struggling new moustache.

"Mom, come on up and see my room," he began, "and you've got to meet some of my profs. We've even planned a dorm tea for you. And, Mom, there is something else I've done. I hope it will be OK."

"Like what?"

"Well, I've invited Don, the leader of our musical group, home for the weekend. Is that OK?"

By the time we left Greenville, we had acquired three more passengers, students needing rides home to Indianapolis.

"Mom, how about letting me drive?" Leon asked.

"Well, OK," I said, "but be careful. It's starting to rain." Leon had received his driver's license the previous year and had shown himself to be a good driver. I slid over and let him take the wheel. As we approached Indianapolis, the interstate clotted with weekend traffic, and in the deepening twilight, tail-lights bled pools of red across the highway ahead of us. It was getting colder. The snow tires hummed noisily, and windshield wipers thumped their steady beat, almost in rhythm with the pattering rain.

"Please, be careful, Leon," I found myself saying as I watched the water glisten like ice on the fences we passed.

Indianapolis cast a dome of light against the low cloud ceiling. On the outskirts, we unloaded our passengers in the cold rain, and then we headed south into the suburb of Greenwood. We could see the distinctive grillwork of the "ORMISO HEIGHTS" sign, marking the entrance to the headquarter complex of OMS International (now One Mission Society) where I worked and lived. In a moment, our big white apartment building appeared in the headlights, smiling a bright welcome.

"Leon, you're home!" Lorna squealed as she flung open the front door. Suddenly she looked older than her fifteen years. With fair skin and honey-blonde hair, she was a striking contrast to her dark-complexioned brother, who towered a full foot above her.

When Leon introduced his friend, Don, as our weekend guest, I detected distress signals coming from Lorna. In a moment, she tugged at my sleeve and eased me into the kitchen.

"Mom," she wailed, "you didn't tell me we were having company. I don't know if I've fixed enough food. What'll I do?"

"It's OK, honey," I soothed. "There'll be plenty. I don't eat much." Lorna placed her creation, a dish of Indian curry, on the table along with a salad and vegetables. We sat down, bowed our heads for grace, and began eating.

Lorna shot a glance at her brother who was cautiously sampling her new dish. "You don't like it," she accused. "I can tell you don't like it."

"No, no. Honestly I do. It's really good."

"No," she insisted, "I can tell. You really don't like it."

The conversation had a comfortable and familiar ring to it. It felt good to have Leon home.

Dinner over, Leon announced that he and Don would drive over to see Leon's girlfriend, Wynoka.

"Hey, Lorna. How about coming along?"

Now that was something. Inviting his kid sister! College was making a real gentleman of Leon, I decided.

"Don't worry, Mom," Leon called out. "We'll just bowl a game or two and be back early. Won't be long."

As the car moved away into the darkness, I noted that it

was still raining, but now it seemed colder. Temperatures were dropping sharply.

It seems somehow incongruous that the days which irrevocably change one's life on earth should be filled with ordinary events: the rising of an ordinary February sun, an office filled with ordinary conversations, the sound of telephones ringing and car doors slamming and friendly hellos and dull rain and, "Leon, I know you really don't like it!"

No, looking back and reliving those final precious moments of earthly time, it still seems wrong that the valley should approach that way. There should be intimations and gentle cautions.

Half an hour later, the doorbell summoned me to the front door to look wonderingly into the face of a blue-uniformed police officer.

"Are you Mrs. Steel?" he began slowly, as though groping for the right words. Or was this a speech he had given before, the words nearly memorized? I cannot be sure.

"Yes, I'm Mrs. Steel."

"Mrs. Steel, do you have a teenage boy about eighteen and a girl a little younger?

"Well, yes, I do," I mumbled.

"Mrs. Steel, it's getting colder. The rain is turning to ice. There has just been an accident on the 37 Bypass. I'm sorry to have to tell you that your children and their friend have just been killed."

Suddenly I felt as if I had been pushed over a high cliff into a wild, seething sea, unable to swim. My mind was creating images: Leon and Lorna in their final moment, as the car spun out of control, and then the crunch of metal against their soft flesh. *It was too much.* The accident which had taken their lives would now surely take mine as well.

But at that very moment, I felt myself in the strong embrace of the Spirit of God. I was being lifted upward, above the cold winter trees, sweetly, securely, into the warm presence of my Father. With a calm, which I instinctively knew had its source from beyond my own being, I heard myself saying, "Officer, I know where they are. They are with God."

Now there would be the phone calls, consoling friends, flowers, "arrangements," and at last the long caravan of cars heading to the familiar plot of ground and newly spaded earth. Here I was walking the valley again – a painful scenario I knew too well. And yet concurrently, in the dark countenance of death, sweet tokens kept coming from my mighty and loving heavenly Father. His love came in great billows, washing over my broken and bleeding heart, bringing again that refreshing comfort to me.

Yea, though I walk through the valley of the shadow of death, I will fear no evil: for thou art with me (Psalm 23:4 KJV). Yes, this was the valley again. I recognized it all right. It comes on you suddenly with a phone call, a knock at the door, the appearance of the messenger, and the word. The first time the word had been "leukemia."

2

LESSONS FROM THE ALCHEMY OF SUFFERING

He was born September 2, 1952, and we named him Daniel Phillip. I was nineteen when Danny was born. Henry and I had been married a little over a year. When expectant mothers fabricate dreams of their firstborn, mentally creating the child they hope for, I would guess that half the women in America would conjure up a child like Danny.

A chubby little guy, he arrived with a head of blond hair, huge blue eyes, and a personality that would charm a cobra. Happy and content with the world, he was usually brimming with laughter, a friend to every creature that came across his path.

By the time he was two, our hometown, Sherwood, Michigan, had adopted Danny as the unofficial town mascot. He was a familiar sight on Main Street of the little village, a big cowboy hat pushed down over his head and a pair of six-guns dangling from his hips. Almost any weekday morning he could be seen sauntering alongside his daddy on their morning trip to the post office. He knew scores of the town folk by name. He greeted strangers and friends alike with a wide grin and childish chatter. "Hi, ya, Mr. Frank," he would call out.

"Hi, ya, Danny. How's the old Lone Ranger doing this morning?"

Looking with eyes full of wonder and awe at our firstborn, Henry had reverently spoken the words, "My son" – words that he had seldom heard from the lips of his own father, except in anger or displeasure. I, too, longed to be the warm and loving mother I had never known.

Not that my mother had been a harsh or unkind person, but she had grown up in hard times and in a family where feelings and conflicts were deeply buried. There was little time for laughter or play. Driving along Route 41, just outside Lowell, Indiana, south of Gary, I can still reflect upon a rusted old windmill, the forlorn landmark on the edge of the Haberlin place, a 200-acre farm that had been in Mother's family for three generations and on which her forebears struggled daily to eke out a modest living. Those were hard times. My parents had eloped in 1930, and I was born three years later in the depths of the Great Depression.

I am sure that in her way Mother had loved us. "I love you," however, was an expression no one ever heard escape her lips. She was not one given to displays of affection, and when Dad would put his burly arms around her slender figure, she would pull away in embarrassment.

Children had come in relentless succession. I arrived two years after Arthur, then came Leonora, my dearest friend and confidant; we were followed by Eugene, Ronnie, Sharon, and Melvin.

School-day mornings at the Stevenson house seemed a nerve-wracking exercise in which Mother, increasingly distraught and furrowed of brow, orchestrated a tense drama designed to move a houseful of wriggling youngsters through a routine of dressing, chores, breakfast, and finally onto the school bus. The approaching bus loomed in her mind as a kind of doomsday machine, perversely designed to prove her an incompetent mother. Each morning featured some small trauma, and repeatedly I climbed exhausted onto the yellow school bus.

All her life, Mother seemed to struggle frantically to keep her world under control. While occasionally recalling her dream of becoming a schoolteacher, she set her mind dutifully to cook three meals a day and labor hours over what seemed to be tons of laundry. The drudgery of it had turned her face into a dour mask of anxiety and joylessness.

By the time I was sixteen, I found myself yearning to get away from home. Mother's burdens were becoming my burdens, and they seemed too heavy. I also felt inhibited and stifled with a mother I could neither talk to nor understand and from whom I felt no affection. I dreamed of doing something for God with my life and wondered who could help me.

But if Mother's personality seemed cold and distant, I found my father's a harbor of warmth and security in the troubled ocean of my growing-up years. By no means perfect, he could be narrow-minded and strict. Yet he possessed a deep devotion to God, a wholesome enthusiasm for life, and unshakable integrity. Everyone who knew him admired him.

Yet, at heart, Dad was a nomad, and he came by his wandering ways naturally. His own father, an original Michigan hillbilly, had come from an unruly gypsy-like clan that never stayed anywhere long enough to put down roots. In the process of acquiring a grade school education, Dad had enrolled in fifteen schools. He passed down to us lurid tales of hunting dogs and porcupines and wild exploits of the Stevensons. "That Stevenson bunch," someone remarked in later years, "if they don't get religion, they'll end up boozers!"

With the Great Depression beginning, Dad had been invited to Indiana by his sister, who had married a young pastor, Lester Lee, and there he met my mother in a home prayer meeting.

They married and then moved to Toledo, Ohio, where Dad set about to look for work – a bleak prospect in 1930. When someone mentioned that the Auto-Lite Company was hiring, he hurried to the employment office, only to discover a line of a hundred other desperate and hopeful applicants. But by seven thirty that evening, with no prospect of a job in sight, all but two of the applicants had gone home. Both were hired, and Dad was one of them.

At Auto-Lite, he proved himself an able and reliable worker, gradually helping pay off the mountain of debts his father had accumulated, while building a small home for Mother and himself. He was amazed at his wife's ability to save money, something unheard of in his family. But as the unions strong-armed their way into the shop, pressuring all the workers to join, something in Dad revolted.

He wanted no part in the union's methods, their drinking parties, or vulgar language. Despite remonstrances of friends, Dad would not budge. Never one to make speeches, when it came to matters of conscience, he was a man of unshakable convictions and unyielding scruples. As a result, he was black-listed by the union and many times passed over for promotions.

When I was seven, we moved to a small, 22-acre farm near Temperance, Michigan. Dad enlarged and remodeled our farm-house to accommodate our ever-increasing clan. The back porch was enclosed to provide living quarters for my grandmother, who lived with us periodically until her death.

Following the construction of our farmhouse, Dad began building other houses and eventually obtained a contractor's license.

Dad could be tough. There were no cash allowances for the Stevenson kids. We earned every cent, and the use of the family automobile was carefully allocated. Yet, to an amazing degree, Dad gave us free rein. Though I doubt that he had ever read a book on child psychology, he was a genius at instilling in us healthy motivation. He taught us a wholesome fear of God, so much so that he seldom had to resort to his own disciplinary measures.

He taught by example. Today, all seven children live productive Christian lives. Two of us, my sister Lea and I, are missionaries, and brothers Eugene and Melvin are ministers.

Dad often appeared happy and easygoing, but resisting his authority meant swift and certain retribution. I learned this for myself one summer afternoon in the potato patch behind the barn. Tired and disenchanted from groveling around in the dirt for potatoes, a family project, I wandered off to amuse myself in other ways. When Dad ordered me back on the job, I clearly indicated I had other ideas. He stood up abruptly, strode over to a nearby tree, and fashioned a switch. Sensing doom, I scurried back into the patch and started digging with fervor. It was a lesson not lost on me. Children find security in tough parents who express clear demands and then enforce them.

But above all, Dad's faith and love proved to be the rudder of my young life. During his own teenage years, when his family lived in Toledo, he was invited to a revival in a small church where sinners were customarily invited to kneel at the altar to "get right with God." At the invitation, he longed to go forward, but shy and timid, he hung back. Finally, someone offered to accompany him, and that night Dad asked Christ into his life. "As I walked home that night," he loved to recount, "the stars were brighter, crisper. I felt a peace I had never known. Even the trees seemed to be singing."

When he told his family what he had done, the response was predictable. "George's got religion," they guffawed. But there was no gainsaying; a radical change had taken place in his life. He had indeed been born again. Later, both parents, his sisters, and three brothers came to Christ.

Dad joined the local church and became a faithful member of the sort that were referred to as "pillars" of the congregation. Family devotions were a regular regimen in our home. Every night after supper, Dad would get out the big, leather-bound, well-thumbed Bible. Then, one by one, each of us would pray, and Dad would lead us in the Lord's Prayer. Dad always prayed in conversational tones, as though on uncomplicated terms with his Lord.

When I reached my twelfth year, there came a growing conviction that I should give myself to God. The moment arrived, not in a church service, but in the quiet of my room. I eased myself down onto the linoleum floor by my bed, confessed every sin I could remember, and asked Jesus into my heart. I was surprised not to feel a rush of emotion as I had expected. In fact, it was nothing like Dad's conversion experience, a fact that troubled me with doubt for years to come.

Was I a Christian? I hoped so. I loved the Lord and had done all I knew to do, and yet I wished I could talk about it with someone, maybe my mother. But she had a faith of her own. I am sure it was a real faith, and yet she never spoke of it. Even her prayers in public were soft, timid utterances, as though she were fearful someone might hear and raise a question or peer disapprovingly into her soul.

But there were things Mother could talk about easily and one of them was saving money. Saving money had been a way of life. Like many other Americans who had learned how to scrounge and scrimp through the Depression years, she never spent a penny unnecessarily. As for clothes, why should anyone need more than a few dresses, she would ask. Something to cover the body and provide reasonable modesty would suffice. After all, as she often informed me, she had only two dresses as a girl.

The issue of clothes was a sore spot with me. It was not simply that I felt I needed more and better clothes. What bothered me was that I was often forced to wear garments quite unlike anything worn by anyone else in my class – long brown stockings, for instance.

"Let's not see any more bare legs around here," Dad admonished.

"But, Dad," I protested tearfully, "no one else in my school wears these awful old stockings. I hate them."

"Yes, but it is winter, and they're good for you."

"But," I wailed, "how would you like to go to work in black silk trousers when everyone else was wearing overalls?"

Apparently my logic, or my tears, were not lost on him, and he proved more understanding than I had given him credit for. Yet my narrow, provincial environment, combined with my emotional estrangement from my mother, seemed increasingly discouraging.

I longed to escape, to go away to school. So during my freshman year, when a youth choir from a small Christian high school and junior college came to our church, I seized the occasion to make my case. "Dad," I said, "I want to go to Spring Arbor to school. I really do." Astonishingly, Mother did not object, and Dad seemed almost pleased. Perhaps it was because his older sister, Dorothy, had graduated from the same school and married a minister.

Thus, my sophomore year found me in a Christian high school in Spring Arbor, Michigan. It was there that I met Henry Steel, a popular young man. He could be loud and brash, yet he exuded charm, and his air of self-confidence, reminiscent of my dad's, attracted me to him.

Henry was a senior. Three years later, after I had finished a year of college and Henry had graduated from junior college, we were married.

With our financial resources exhausted and no prospect of help from either of our families, we decided to move to

Temperance, work, and save money for a year so Henry could continue college. We purchased a small trailer.

I found a secretarial job at a plant in Toledo that manufactured atomizers. Henry worked at Willys-Overland and assisted Dad in contracting. At the same time, he served as youth minister in my home church, now pastored by a dynamic young man, Larry Burr, who was to play a key role in the future course of our lives.

Early the next year, I discovered I was pregnant. As summer came, the conference superintendent asked Henry to take the pastorate of a small church in Sherwood, Michigan. After much prayer, Henry accepted. For the present, at least, his college degree would have to wait.

It was September when Henry first drove me to Sherwood. The little town, midway between Battle Creek and Jackson, had once been a thriving industrial center, boasting numerous factories, a high school, a railway station, even a college. But Sherwood, failing to keep pace with changing times, had dwindled into a sleepy village. Huge oak trees, heavy with leaves, draped the quiet neighborhood. We drove past an old gentleman shuffling slowly along the all-but-deserted Main Street. He seemed somehow to symbolize that half-forgotten hamlet, old and weary and having no place to go.

Two church buildings fronted on Main Street. The larger of the two, the Methodist Church, had long since been closed. Its dilapidated steeple now sheltered a small flock of pigeons. Across the street stood the smaller Free Methodist Church, a building distinguished by two small front doors that were reminiscent of old Shaker dwellings. This was the church to which we had been appointed. It was, in fact, the oldest building of our denomination in Michigan. Conference leaders had been proposing that the church be disbanded and the building turned into a museum.

Henry drove past the church to the edge of town and turned into a narrow drive that led to a shabby house. "This is it," he announced without emotion. "Our new home." I slowly surveyed the lumpy shingles, the broken windows, and the tangle of weeds that edged up against the front steps. I felt a lump rising in my throat. "Really? Henry," I whispered, "is this it?"

There was a long pause, and then he grinned impishly and started the car. On down the street he turned into a driveway. There stood a frame house with a flat wood porch, but this house was newly painted with windows that glistened. Even the lawn was freshly mowed. Still sputtering, I hardly noticed how old it was. Already it had a "homey" feel to it.

Danny was born on September 2, and ten days later we moved into the Sherwood parsonage. The money we had saved for college went into furnishing the house. We rummaged through second-hand stores until we found living room furniture consisting of a huge, red velvet couch and some faded, overstuffed chairs. An ancient, well-scarred table went into the dining room. After buying beds, there was just enough money left for a washing machine and refrigerator.

The Sunday morning offering, our salary, rarely exceeded $40. Here was a chance for us to prove Matthew 6:33: *Seek first his kingdom and his righteousness, and all these things will be given to you as well* (NIV). If we would really seek first the kingdom of God, his promise was that "these things" would be added unto us, and there were plenty of "these things."

The expenses piled up. The baby needed diapers and an increasing supply of baby food to satisfy his growing appetite. Then came heating fuel, gasoline, tires, car payments, insurance premiums, to say nothing of groceries. Usually, by the time the weekend arrived, we were totally insolvent.

But repeatedly, God provided. Sometimes it would be an anonymous offering slipped into our mailbox or the fee from a wedding or funeral. Church people would appear at the door unannounced with a basket of produce, a package of beef, or some chickens.

As the congregation grew, the board fashioned a budget. Our salary was increased, and a car allowance was paid for visitation and church work. From our hearts we sang, "Praise God from whom all blessings flow."

Meanwhile, the little Sherwood church was experiencing a resurrection of such magnitude that church leaders all over the state were taking notice. The original congregation of twenty-five to thirty had doubled and doubled and doubled again. Henry and I dreamed of dozens of schemes to increase church attendance, and to each of them, Henry brought his soaring vitality.

No one in Sherwood could remember anything quite like it. People who had previously shown no interest in religion came out of curiosity to observe the phenomenon. Tirelessly, we worked with young people, began Sunday school training seminars, planned Sunday school promotions, and organized a quiz team that took second place in the state finals.

Together, we spent hours brainstorming how to use the talents of each person who came to the church. The people kept coming. Chairs were put in the aisles to accommodate the overflow. When Sunday morning attendance reached a hundred and fifty in the little church, it was clear something had to be done. And, as usual, Henry and I began dreaming up ideas.

Although the old Methodist Church across the street had been condemned as a fire hazard, Henry learned that it was not beyond repair. He made an offer to the denomination of $1,000, which the leadership promptly accepted. Renovation would cost a little more, about $6,000, and Henry erected a huge thermometer in front of the church to chart the progress of the building fund. His slogan was "Build for Tomorrow."

Gradually the old building underwent a remarkable

transformation. Volunteers came to wield a paintbrush, a hammer, wash windows, scrub floors, or pull weeds. The women and I prepared potluck dinners on the lawn. My father, an experienced builder, helped rebuild the crumbling belfry. The pigeons would have to find a new home.

As the work progressed in Sherwood, we agreed that Henry should get on with his schooling. This meant additional expenses plus the cost of commuting fifty miles several days a week to Spring Arbor. There seemed only one way to make ends meet: I would have to work. I found a job as a secretary in the Douglas Manufacturing plant in nearby Bronson. This meant leaving Danny each morning in the care of his "grandmothers," church women who offered to care for him while I worked.

As I pulled in front of Mrs. Masters' or Mrs. Myers' home each morning, the first rays of sun would just begin to touch the sky with orange and pink. "Good-bye, Danny. Be a good boy. I love you."

Backing out of the drive, I could hear his laughter. I held back the tears as I drove away. Often, as I was punching at the typewriter, my thoughts flitted to Henry, to the church, to a dozen activities that required my attention, to meals that needed planning, and then to Danny, my precious Danny, not yet a year old. What kind of mother was I? Other women were raising my child. But this was only a temporary arrangement, I consoled myself. Before too long, Henry would have his degree, and I would be home with Danny. Life would slow down and settle into a comfortable, manageable routine.

I was approaching my twentieth birthday, the age when most girls are enjoying the full bloom of youthful energy. But I was exhausted, stretched to the breaking point, trying just to keep pace with my dynamo of a husband and my own ambitious ideals. "Lord," I would pray, "just give me strength to get through one more day."

Weekends, instead of providing some rest from my demanding schedule, usually meant an even more frenzied pace. The parsonage seemed to be a continuous open house, a hub of ceaseless activity. This was the way I had always wanted my home to be, but now I was tired, so tired, and there seemed never enough time to do what needed to be done.

I remember one Saturday morning after mopping floors, straightening the house, doing the week's wash, and finding a few moments to play with Danny – just savoring being at home for a change – I flopped down on the sofa, totally spent. With lunch hardly over, one of the church members dropped in, bringing with him a big apple pie.

People seldom stopped by the Steel parsonage for only a minute. Henry was a good listener, a brilliant conversationalist with a flair for entertaining people. The bearer of the pie was hardly out the door when a delegation of men involved in the prison ministry appeared for fellowship. Now the phone was ringing – it was our new director of music calling to ask if it was all right for him to eat dinner with us.

By nine thirty that evening, I was still in the kitchen, finishing the last of the supper dishes when Henry poked his head in.

"Valetta," he asked, "could you type up my sermon outline and give me some feedback?"

"I can't. I just can't," I pleaded. "I still have the bulletin to do and the hymns need to be chosen."

It was 11:30 when I finished the stencil and began cranking the old mimeograph machine. The ink was cold and blotched. I noticed a misspelled word and decided to ignore it. Finally I tumbled into bed, but it seemed only moments until the alarm rang, prodding me up and into another day of ceaseless demands.

About five minutes before church, Henry glanced at the bulletin. "Valetta," he snapped, "there is a big mistake here. How could you let this happen?" The dike of my emotional control and spiritual serenity broke.

"OK, OK," I shot back. "You can do it yourself if all you are ever going to do is criticize."

As soon as I had spoken those words, I regretted them and wished desperately I could somehow snatch them back. What had happened to the inward poise in which I took such pride? I was growing touchy and irritable. Almost every day, it seemed, I had to ask God and others to forgive me for my attitude.

Henry's counsel too often seemed like preaching to me. Why couldn't he meet my needs? Why wasn't he sensitive to my hurts, to my weariness? I had given him my life, my future, my dreams, and now when I needed him most, he didn't understand. Somehow he couldn't help me. Did he really care?

"You don't love me," I shouted one day. "Why can't you understand and help me rather than preach at me?"

My words brought a look of stunned disbelief. "Of course I love you," he said in a voice that seemed suddenly low and pained. "I can't imagine a day without you. For you to even think that hurts and disappoints me. Valetta, sometimes I just don't understand you."

Gradually the Lord revealed to me that a great deal of the pressure and anxiety I was feeling was the result of a vain and hopeless effort to conform to the role of "model wife" – a standard I imagined my gifted husband demanded of me. One morning, as I waited on my knees with my Bible open, the Lord spoke to me through the Psalms. *It is better to trust in the* LORD *than to put confidence in man* (Psalm 118:8 KJV). God showed me that I had made an idol of my husband. Now, in the light of God's Word, I saw Henry as a man – handsome, responsible, caring, demanding, and yet not perfect, not all knowing, not all powerful. I must put my ultimate trust in God and not in man. It was a lesson I was just beginning to learn and would have to learn in a far deeper way in the months and years ahead.

Still, life moved on at a relentless pace, and for Henry there was no letting up. Every success surged him on to greater challenges. He purchased a second-hand printing press, rented a vacant bank building in town, and set up a print shop. It was not enough that Henry Steel was a student, minister, pastor, youth leader, church builder, baseball player, to say nothing of father and husband; he now aspired to head a small publishing enterprise.

While the congregation responded with mounting enthusiasm to the vision and charisma of this young man, his wife was foundering along in his wake, somehow trying to establish order in the turmoil of life. I seemed to be climbing a steep mountain, but I told myself, "Once I reach the summit, the going will be easier – it will be downhill from there. There will be times to relax and lead a normal life." And then one day that winter, I realized with a curious mixture of joy and dread that I was pregnant again.

I quit my job in Bronson, and our second son was born October 19. Dark in complexion, he bore a striking resemblance to his father.

"Let's name him Henry," I suggested. "Oh, no, you don't," my husband protested. "We are not going to saddle the kid with a name like Henry." Finally, we arrived at a compromise. He would be called Leon Henry. For me, having another baby meant back to the nursery and the routine of handling diapers. But I found some degree of comfort in all this. Life would actually be simpler for me as fewer demands are made of new mothers. Two years and one month separated Danny and Leon. Danny would have a playmate and Leon a big brother to initiate him into the mysteries and adventures of boyhood.

The small earthquake that was taking place in Sherwood

had not failed to attract the attention of our church leadership. Moreover, Henry was rapidly gaining a reputation as one of the most exciting young preachers in the denomination. It was no surprise when a phone call from church headquarters came one evening, inviting Henry to be the official youth delegate at the general conference. *This would be a good time,* I told myself, *to get away for a few days.* I would take Danny and Leon to visit my parents in Temperance.

When I returned home though, I noticed that Danny seemed irritable and crotchety; he seemed to be in discomfort. He would start crying for no reason. One morning as I glanced out a kitchen window, I noticed him struggling with his tricycle. He seemed to have difficulty manipulating the handlebars. "Mommy," he cried out, "my arm hurts."

Putting the children in the car, I drove to nearby Coldwater to consult the doctor. After examining Danny, Dr. Mooi, a family friend, looked puzzled. "I am afraid there may be something wrong with the bone," he said. "I'd like to do a biopsy tomorrow."

When I got home, I called Henry, and he returned home that same evening. "I shared our concern for Danny with the whole conference," he told me. "They are all praying for us."

When we arrived at the hospital the next morning, we were directed down a long hall to a small emergency center. A blood test would precede the biopsy. Danny screamed as the nurse pricked his finger with a scalpel and caused blood to spurt. Then we waited for hours, it seemed.

Finally Dr. Mooi appeared, beckoning us into his office. "We are canceling the biopsy because we believe we have already diagnosed the problem," he said. Then, slowly and in measured, professional tones, he went on. "The white blood count is very high, and we suspect that your son has acute lymphatic leukemia. However, we are hoping our diagnosis is wrong, and we would like you to take Danny to Ann Arbor University Hospital."

There was a long, awkward pause. Then in a gentle and subdued voice, Dr. Mooi continued. "Telling you this is one of the
hardest things I have ever had to do. We don't know why many
children from good homes develop this disease. Unfortunately,
it is not curable at this time. All we can do is offer you treatments that could extend his time to five or six months, maybe
more." His voice trailed off. "Or maybe we'll find a cure."

We sat there stunned, struggling to take in the reality of
what Dr. Mooi had said. And yet, at the same time, we somehow
wanted to erase the whole conversation from our consciousness.
Surely these words had not been spoken to us. He was speaking
about someone else, not our son, not Danny. These things happen only to other people in faraway places – people you read
about in newspapers, strangers, or perhaps even people in the
church – but not to you.

Leukemia. The word was familiar enough to me. I had read
it many times in magazines and books. Those who have known
its victims speak the word in hushed tones, freighted with pity
or horror. This was the blood disease without a cure. Increasing
debility leading to a slow, painful death: that was leukemia. But
it was a disease that happened to other people.

As we climbed into our old Ford and drove to Ann Arbor,
a thread of hope lingered. The doctor had not been absolutely
certain of his diagnosis. That was the whole point of this trip;
that was why we were going to Ann Arbor. Doctors are often
mistaken. It happens every day. There was a chance, possibly
a good chance, that the whole diagnosis was a big mistake. In
a few hours, we would awaken from this nightmare and drive
home with Danny between us, praising the Lord it was all over.

When we arrived in the parking lot in Ann Arbor, we walked
into a huge octopus-like building with its many wings stretching out like tentacles in every direction. We were directed to
a spacious waiting room, alive with color, obviously designed

and decorated for children. Scattered about were toys and Dr. Seuss books on undersized tables.

The room was full of youngsters, most of them apparently normal. I soon learned, however, that they too were on death's row under the sentence of that terrible disease.

In the examining room, the nurse reached for Danny's finger and made a quick incision. Danny screamed, and each childish wail found an echo in my own wounded spirit and brought a huge lump to my throat. *We will love him so much and take such good care of him,* I thought. *Certainly he will be different. He will get well. We'll find the best physicians in the world, and, of course, God will help.* Soon enough we got the report, which only confirmed Dr. Mooi's diagnosis – leukemia. Apart from a miracle, Danny had no more than a few months to live.

I've tried many times to analyze the phenomenon – how a single moment, a single word, can forever alter the shape of one's world. The mind struggles to comprehend, yet it revolts. The heart will not accept what reason insists is fact. Then, slowly, at intervals, the facts begin to seep down from the numbed brain into the heart, bringing a kind of paralysis. At the same time comes a vague, nagging sense of guilt. *Why me? Why us?* are the questions that intrude again and again. *Where did we fail? Was there something we could have done that we didn't do? Is God punishing us?*

When we returned home, bearing in our arms our firstborn, who was now under the sentence of death, something happened that illustrated the tremendous courage and unselfishness of my husband. As we pulled into Sherwood, Henry clapped his hand to his forehead and said, "Valetta, the baseball game tonight! I forgot all about it, and we have the equipment in the trunk of the car." At the field, we found the team waiting. When they heard the tragic diagnosis, it was suggested that the game be called off.

"Called off?" echoed Henry. "I should say not. We'll go right ahead and play it, and since I'm your star player, don't tell me I shouldn't play either." He did play. It was typical of Henry, never allowing his personal sorrow to cast a shadow upon the joy of another. He looked upon burdening others with his pain as selfishness.

Though Danny was now very sick, the doctors agreed it would be best for him to stay home and be cared for as an outpatient, returning to the hospital every two weeks for observation and treatment. As we traveled the long miles back and forth to the Ann Arbor hospital, leaving Leon behind in the care of Grandmother Myers, the old Ford became a kind of sanctuary for us. God in the presence of the Holy Spirit was with us in a very precious way.

We comforted one another with our recent gleanings from the Word, insights God had given us into the meaning of life and death. Up to this point, death had seemed always remote, a transition relegated to the distant future. This was our first trip through the valley. Someone has said that life is always seen most clearly in the face of death. It is true. In that dark valley, the shadows show more perfectly the true arrangement of life's terrain, the substance of reality.

In the weeks that followed, we kept constant vigil over our stricken child. Was he in pain? Was he losing weight? "Danny will have no resistance to infection," the doctors had warned us. Antibiotics would help only temporarily, and, above all, he had to be kept from catching colds and the flu. Danny came to understand and accept his condition without self-pity, and his spirit touched us deeply.

The only time he did not cooperate was when the nurses approached for the routine blood tests. "I don't want you to take my blood," he would scream, and my heart ached to spare him the ordeal. At times he would look at me with solemn eyes, now bigger than ever against his paling skin. "When will I get well, Mommy?" he would ask. And I would turn away in silence. I had no words to formulate an answer.

We set up a bed for Danny in the dining room, and this big room, which had so recently been the command center for Henry's plethora of church activities, now took on the appearance of a hospital room. We had begun a solemn countdown of days that would bring us to the last fleeting moments of this precious life that had brought us so much sunshine. That shine was fading away. Yet overshadowing those days was the heavenly Presence, gently infusing us with the mysterious hope that is the birthright of every believer: resurrection. That doctrine to which we had always paid lip service was now coming clear.

It is the curious nature of leukemia and other forms of cancer to periodically go into remission. For a time, Danny responded to therapy. Some of his energy returned, bringing with it a wistful, wild hope that maybe the diagnosis had been wrong. Or was God answering our prayers with a divine miracle of healing? It seemed too much to hope for. One afternoon after his nap, I watched Danny struggle to pull himself erect in his crib. Turning a bright face to me, he cried, "Mommy, see, I'm getting better."

"Danny," I whispered to comfort myself as much as him, "Jesus loves you very much, and he will always be with you."

When the remissions came, providing a brief reprieve from the relentless march of the disease, a slight recovery of strength would come to Danny. These were golden hours we savored to the fullest. I would strap on Danny's six-guns, find the battered cowboy hat, and soon it would be time for cowboys and Indians again. Henry had bought him an oversized plastic bat. The two of them would tumble out on the lawn for "baseball." As I stood watching from the window, their shouts and laughter came to my ears with a terrible sweetness.

We were learning something new about the preciousness of time. With the doctor's words, "a few months," we had begun mentally to tick off the days. We could no longer think of Danny's life, our time together with him, as stretching out into a distant future. We could no longer project in our mind's eye scenes of childhood, teenage years, college, adulthood. In a moment, our perspective had changed. Time now was seen as a priceless commodity, so fragile and fleeting. How important that we treasure every hour with our son.

It was as though the joys of a normal life span were being distilled and poured into a few dwindling golden days. Thus, strange as it may seem, those last months were studded with good times, laughter, and fun. When Danny was able to respond, how willingly I would drop everything. I would think, I can't let this opportunity pass.

Gradually, I began to understand that this is the way one should view every moment, every day of his life, as an infinitely precious commodity. How often in our frenzied plans for the future are we too busy for the present? As I study the life of our Lord, I am impressed that there was, as one writer puts it, a certain "large sense of leisure" about him. He had time for people. When he saw that people needed him, he zeroed in on them, giving of himself without worrying about time.

Parents often wish they had learned Christ's example when their children were growing up: during those tumultuous teenage years when eternal moments were passing. But they were busy with a hundred other things, and now they look back with regret on hours, days, and years that cannot be recovered.

For us, the good times stood out in bold relief – bright jewels against the dark background of pain and weakness. Each remission inevitably was followed by a fresh onslaught of the malignancy, so irrevocably entrenched in our oldest son's little body. While Leon thrived, Danny wasted away. Pale and quiet, he lay on his bed and turned large pitiful eyes to us in silent pleas for help. His small face grew puffed, and his skin took on a shiny appearance. His stomach became distended. A painful urinary infection developed that strong medication could not cure. It seemed we were continually making fruitless trips with Danny to the hospital.

The disease often produced a tremendous thirst that nothing seemed to quench. Through long night hours, I often sat, weeping and praying, with Danny on my lap. One night I cried to God, "Lord, was it like this at Calvary?" Then I thought, *You went through it for me, so surely you must love me and understand my pain.*

When Christians go through experiences like this one, we expect ourselves to remember all the sermons we have ever heard on the meaning of suffering and recall all the books we have read that explain God's providential ways. We are to appreciate that through these strange circumstances that make up the fiery ordeal, there is a purging, a stretching, an enriching. All of these things *are* taking place, of course. A day did come when I could look back and say, "Yes, Lord. Thank you. I can see your purposes now. I think I can understand at least a part of the meaning of it all."

But I have to be honest in saying that as we sat there through those long night hours, trying to quench our son's unquenchable thirst, trying to soothe and bring relief; when I stood at my kitchen sink, my hands in dishwater, my tormented heart lifted to God with salty tears running down my cheeks – I wasn't seeing the full picture. What I was doing was asking God for his strength, his grace, just for that moment, that hour, to get me through that day.

I began to grasp an important fact. God does not ask us to bear the whole burden at once. He asks only that we live through that moment, that hour, that day, and his promise is that *as thy days, so shall thy strength be* (Deuteronomy 33:25 KJV). I learned not to ask God for big, earth-shaking events. I would think, *Here is our little Sherwood community, and these people are praying for me – praying that somehow I'll get through this ordeal and that I'll be a witness for Christ. Lord, don't let me let you down.*

Later, someone asked me if there ever was a time when I thought I just couldn't take it anymore. I could honestly answer, "No." My reason was simple.

Psalm 1 describes the person who is *like a tree planted by rivers of water.* Not only does he *bringeth forth his fruit in his season* but *his leaf also shall not wither.* The psalmist tells us that this person meditates upon the Word of God, day and night.

A nice picture. During the trying times with Danny, I was discovering in my life this profound truth: meditating on the Word of God had made me strong like the psalmist's tree. As a teenager, I had tried to imitate my father and his love for the Bible. When I went away to school at Spring Arbor, I had determined that no matter how busy my daily schedule became, nothing would crowd out my time alone with the Lord. Though I occasionally missed my devotions, God enabled me, for the most part, to keep my pledge to end each day in the Word with him.

It was never my habit to read long passages of Scripture at one time, but rather to take shorter portions, meditate upon them, turn them over and over in my mind. The Holy Spirit seemed to guide me to certain passages that became precious favorites. I marked verses that seemed to apply to my life and returned to them often.

And now I was discovering that in the withering furnace of affliction, my leaf was not withering. But those precious streams of living water kept rising up into my heart, refreshing me daily, hourly, moment by moment.

Through the centuries, God's suffering people have turned

often to the book of Job. And for me, Job came alive in a new way, as did the prophets Jeremiah, Isaiah, and Daniel, whose suffering foreshadowed the agony of Christ. They became my companions as I walked through the valley.

For the first time, I could understand and truly appreciate the tortured cry of Jesus in the Garden of Gethsemane: *Father, if thou be willing, remove this cup from me* (Luke 22:42 KJV). God's Word kept me from unwarranted guilt and negative thinking, leading me out of a maze of depression, and always with the assurance that, in spite of everything, God was still in control. He was upholding the universe and me.

As I look at many young people in our society today, one message keeps coming to me: here are lives out of control. They don't want to be controlled because control requires responsibility. So they have adopted lifestyles and attitudes of irresponsibility.

They communicate a philosophy that says the world is out of control, and here is where the Christian can give unwavering testimony. Once we are in God's kingdom, we acknowledge that he is King and he is in control, even when something happens that seems impossible to bear. For me, the Word brought acceptance, comfort, poise, and a certainty that in spite of everything, *he guards the lives of his faithful ones* (Psalm 97:10 NIV).

As medical bills mounted, the church was eager to help us bear the financial burden. We became objects of a special outpouring of sympathy and love. Gifts appeared regularly in the mail. Nearly every week, someone had a scheme for raising money for Danny. There were bake sales, flower sales, car washes. God began to show us something very important and beautiful about the body of Christ. Whenever God's people meet together in any communion, they bring with them all their humanity, weaknesses, and yes, their sins.

Some in the church had come from different denominational backgrounds. We didn't see eye-to-eye on everything. An "old guard" had viewed with suspicion some of the "innovations" Henry had instituted. Differences of opinion had left a legacy of small hurts and misunderstandings. But now, with the shadow of death on our home, those petty problems seemed unworthy of mention as differences faded and then disappeared. Through the alchemy of suffering, our hearts were fused into that sweet unity that the songwriter must have had in mind when he wrote, "the fellowship of kindred minds is like to that above."

But beyond the bond that suffering creates between God's people, I felt a new kind of bond, a oneness with all humanity, because *all* humanity suffers. I began to realize that no one you look at, ever, hasn't in some way been touched by pain and sorrow. It was not that I had been singled out by God for some special ordeal. All over the world, people live in various stages of suffering. People are in the process of losing loved ones. There are thousands of others who have lost two-year-old children.

Each time we took Danny to the Ann Arbor hospital for treatment, we lined up with seventy or eighty other families. It dawned on me there that I was not all that unique. I, too, was part of the fabric of humanity's dark side, its sin, its curse, its suffering and death. Suffering was giving me a new perspective on life, and at the same time it was convincing me more than ever that the greatest need of man is to know the One who said, *I am the resurrection, and the life: he that believeth in me, though he were dead, yet shall he live* (John 11:25 KJV).

While I was going through *my* Gethsemane, Henry was going through his. But at times, it seemed as though we were traveling different roads. Often, suffering creates special ties between husband and wife, and I am sure that Danny's did for us, though not in the way one might suppose. Henry had grown up without a mother and estranged from his father; he found it difficult to bare his heart to anyone, even to his wife.

In the darkest moments of his life, he sometimes seemed

imprisoned in a shell of silence. We usually went to the Word, prayed, and agonized separately. Often the first inkling I had of what was going through Henry's mind came when I typed his sermon notes. The inner turmoil, which he found so difficult to share with any individual, he somehow found the freedom to speak of when he stood in the pulpit.

I particularly remember one Sunday morning when Henry revealed that during the long nights he had tearfully demanded of God, "Why, why have you taken this son for whom we have such plans? This son whom we consecrated to you?"

Then Henry went on to speak of God's answer to the question: "Is it not enough that I understand and have given my own Son over to such pain? Is it not enough that I care about your grief?"

That night a reply was wrung from Henry's tormented heart. "It is enough, Lord."

In February, six months after the first signs of the disease, Danny suffered a brain hemorrhage. Now he could no longer speak clearly. Though his mind was still alert, his muscles would not respond as he strained to formulate familiar sounds that would express his need. The eyes, so large and blue against his pale, thin face, pleaded for understanding.

Then one morning, soon after, we were startled to note the absence of the familiar sounds with which Danny usually greeted us. Quickly, we made our way into the dining room. We stood speechless. Danny was no longer there. Only the pale, wasted shell of what had been his earthly house remained. Our son was, at last, at peace.

The little town of Sherwood fell unusually quiet as word of Danny's death spread from post office to gas station to telephone party line. While the town mourned with us, we, for the first time, undertook the melancholy chores encompassed by the term "funeral arrangements" – the selection of a burial plot, a headstone, and a small casket. The satin-lined box, had it a happier function, would have been described as cute, but as the final resting place of a two-year-old child, its tiny dimensions seemed a cruel reminder of the power of death.

On March 23, a cold, blustery day, we gathered at the church for Danny's funeral. We who had so often mourned with others were mourners ourselves this day. It was a strange sensation, unreal, as though we were going through motions while in a trance or being manipulated like puppets. Was this really happening to us?

After the little box was lowered into the spaded earth, church people and friends climbed into their cars and faded off into the landscape. We stood almost alone with our son, Leon. The wind was blowing hard now, whipping a cold drizzle into our faces. Standing beside us was our music director, Byron Hosmer.

"What would you like to do tonight?" Byron asked softly.

"How can we best think about heaven?" Henry responded in a surprisingly strong voice.

"I know," Byron said, "why don't we take in an orchestra concert at Battle Creek?"

So we drove to the concert hall that night and listened to the violins and trumpets. They reminded us of God's great orchestra that, one day, we will hear play heavenly music. They also reminded us that Danny was already there.

3

A Second
Countdown to Tragedy

On campus, Henry was the kind of person who was not easily ignored. He was a senior – loud, cocky, a varsity baseball player. He seemed bent on proving that he was a man, tough, in control. But whatever his faults, it was generally agreed that Henry Steel was fun, a guy everyone liked.

Above all, Henry loved his Lord unashamedly. He had declared himself a ministerial student, and those who had heard him preach affirmed that he possessed unusual power and eloquence for so young a man. Already he was in constant demand to supply pulpits in the area. *Someday,* I told myself, *I would like to date Henry Steel.*

The following year, Henry had intended to enroll in Spring Arbor Junior College, though he was unable to do so. Without assistance from home, he could not pay his tuition and had been forced to drop out for a year to work. He found a job in an automobile plant in Flint.

To help with expenses, he had his sights on a partial scholarship offered by the denomination to the youth who solicited the largest number of subscriptions to the church youth magazine. In the competition, Henry's closest competitor was a determined young lady from Temperance – me. With our church's energetic new pastor, Larry Burr, urging me on, I felt certain I would land the prize.

The following fall, my senior year in high school, I was standing in the registration line, scanning the scores of new and unfamiliar faces, when I saw Henry. Feeling inexplicably excited, I summoned all my courage and called his name. "Henry, Henry Steel." He whirled around, and his eyes met mine. I had learned that Henry was my closest rival in the magazine contest but I had not yet heard the results. "Who won the scholarship?" I asked. "Do you know?"

"Valetta," he said softly, seeming somehow different from the brash senior who had graduated the year before, "if it weren't for that scholarship, I would still be working at Fisher Body. The Lord did so many great things to supply my financial needs. I know he wants me here in college." Then he added gently, "I'm sorry, though, that you lost."

"I'm really glad you won it, Henry," I replied, with a sincerity that surprised me. "I really am."

Back in the dorm, I finished unpacking, excitedly reporting the events of the summer to my roommate, Margaret. Then I headed for the dining hall. At the front steps, I noticed Henry.

"Hi." I smiled. "How are things going?"

"Oh, fine," he replied. Then he shattered our small talk with a question. "Valetta, how about getting together tonight for the opening reception?"

Henry Steel asking me for a date? I struggled to conceal my excitement, paused a moment as though pondering the question, and then in a voice that I desperately hoped sounded calm and mature beyond my sixteen years, I replied, "Sure, that would be great. What time should we meet?"

I could hardly wait to get back to my room. "Margaret," I

gasped, "you won't believe what just happened! Henry Steel is back, and he just asked me for a date tonight. I am so excited! I think he is the neatest guy on campus."

The reception that evening took place on the broad stretch of lawn behind the administration building. As we walked toward the refreshment table, the breeze felt suddenly cool on my skin. Instinctively, I clasped my arms around me for warmth. Henry paused in the middle of a story about his work at Fisher Body, took off his big sweater, and draped it around my shoulders. Engulfed in his blue cardigan, my face turned red.

"It was so stupid of me to forget a sweater," I stammered.

"What?" Henry responded in mock offense. "You mean you don't like my sweater?"

Soon it was curfew time for high school students. "Well, this will be the end," I told myself. Henry, by asking me out, had made one gallant gesture to his rival in the scholarship contest. The magic spell was about to break. Tomorrow, classes would begin, and then it would be back to reality.

"Good night, Henry," I said.

"One question before 'good night,'" he replied. "How about having dinner with me Friday night?"

"OK, well, sure, I would be glad to," I stammered again, trying not to show the surge of pleasure I felt.

As I climbed up the steps to my room and looked over my schedule, I realized with some regret that I had not left much time for dating. I was carrying a load of five subjects, singing in a mixed quartet, working part time for the school registrar, and practicing basketball two nights a week. My unscheduled time that remained would have to be devoted to study, and plenty of it, if I wanted to keep up my grade point average.

Several weeks later, after turning down Henry's invitation to "get together" for the third night in a row, explaining that I had to study, Henry looked at me disapprovingly. "Why do you have to be such a slave to your studies?" he argued. "What's the point? School is not the real world, you know. Once you walk out the door, you'll discover what life is all about, and that's when what you have really learned will count, not whether you got straight As."

Unless I studied hard, I could never preserve my straight-A record. The thought of letting my grades slip frightened me because my academic record spelled a kind of security to me – a security I very much needed. "Learning is an important process," I answered. "Besides, it helps one develop discipline." I had to admit, though, that in more than one class my only motive to study was the pursuit of another A.

Not easily discouraged, Henry had other schemes that would offer opportunity for us to see each other. He suggested my quartet accompany him Sunday evenings to a little church where he sometimes preached. When I played basketball, Henry would organize an impromptu pep squad consisting of his buddies to provide vociferous encouragement. With the sound of his voice rising in unrestrained enthusiasm above the others, my face would turn red to the delight of my teammates. One Friday that fall, as our quartet left for a long weekend of meetings, Larry, a tall senior in our group, turned to me and with a sly twinkle in his eye said, "You know, Valetta, Henry has another girl back home."

The next day after dinner, Henry suggested that we go for a walk. The October sun felt warm, and the leaves were turning. We strolled past a few quiet houses to a small field. Henry paused and looked at the ground. "There is something I feel I need to tell you," he began slowly. "You see, there is this girl back home in my church in Flint, and now, well, I'm starting to care about you. I am asking God to show me his will. So I have decided to go home this weekend. I just wanted you to know that."

Since Larry had told me about the "other girl," I too had been praying that if Henry's friendship was in God's plan, he would show me. "Henry, all that I want is God's perfect will for our lives," I said. "Let's pray that God will guide you in whatever decision you make as you go home." We bowed our heads and prayed. I then pondered Psalm 138:8: *The Lord will work out his plans for my life—for your loving-kindness, Lord, continues forever* (TLB).

The following week, we walked past a few quiet houses to a vacant lot. The wind sent shivers through me, and I stepped up the pace. Henry reached for my arm. "Let's stop," he said, and then looking intently into my eyes he began to speak softly. "I believe I care for you a lot," he said, "so I have broken up with the girl back home. Could we become steady friends like regular dates and all?"

I paused, suddenly aware of my heart thumping wildly, and I struggled to form a suitable response. All that came out was a simple, "Yes, Henry, of course." Somehow, I could not yet tell him how much I cared.

Then he took my hands in his and drew me toward him. "May I kiss you?" he asked.

Two years later on a sweltering July day, we were married in my home church in Temperance. It was a simple ceremony, but the little church was packed. By this time, I had completed my freshman year of college, just one year behind Henry. Our financial resources were all but depleted.

We moved into a small trailer on the outskirts of Lambertville, determined to work a year, save our money, and continue our schooling at Roberts Wesleyan College at North Chili, New York. I found a secretarial job, working for the DeVilbiss Company, and Henry worked at WillysOverland, helped Dad with building projects, and served as our church's youth pastor.

Our minister at this time, Larry Burr, was to prove a key

influence in Henry's development. Energetic and creative, Larry had broken out of the mold of provincial denominationalism and caught a vision for the world. Missions to him was not merely a project of the Ladies' Auxiliary, represented by somber, drably garbed spinsters presiding over a table of native dolls and Oriental curiosities. No, missions was the greatest task in the world, the enterprise nearest the heart of God, something to get excited about and to give one's life for. How his vision would become Henry's vision, and one day so alter the course of our lives, I could never have at that time imagined.

Our Sherwood pastorate followed. And after Danny's death and the completion of our third year at Sherwood, Henry and I both sensed the nudge of the Holy Spirit. Certainly, this was the time for Henry to finish his college education.

We spent that summer, following our resignation, in Temperance, where Henry worked for my father in his lumber business. It was a delightful hiatus between the hectic routine of the parsonage and what we thought would be the beginning of a new school year. There were leisurely hours with the family, time for recreation and rest. Oh, how we needed rest!

Then one afternoon, a delegation of laymen from a church in Kalamazoo pulled up in front of Dad's business. Henry had held a series of evangelistic meetings in the church a short time earlier and recognized the spokesman of the committee, a man named Wilson Hibbard. After some pleasantries, Wilson disclosed the purpose of their visit.

"Henry, our pastor is about to retire, and we are looking for a replacement," he began. "We've prayed about it, and we are convinced that you are the man."

"Gentlemen," Henry replied, "I'm honored by your request, but we have already enrolled in a college. In fact, our furniture has been moved to an apartment there."

After the men left, I saw Henry standing strangely quiet with his head down. Slowly he turned to me. "I answered them before even praying," he said. Then with a sigh, he added, "Valetta, I have a strange impression that God wants me in Kalamazoo. I feel uneasy about going back to school. Somehow, I sense the time is short, as though for some reason it is important that I get back into the work."

We agreed to put out a kind of fleece. "Lord," Henry said, "if this impression, which humanly speaking does not make sense, is really of you, lead the committee from the Kalamazoo church to approach me again."

Two weeks later, a long-distance call came from Wilson Hibbard. "Henry," he began, "I'm calling to see if you will reconsider your decision."

In September we moved to Kalamazoo. Living with us now were my sister Leonora (Lea), who was in nurse's training, and our youth minister, Frank Gorsline, who had found Christ through Henry's ministry in Sherwood. Kalamazoo, peopled largely by stolid families of Dutch descent, was inviting, clean, and distinguished for its economic prosperity and low rate of unemployment. It had been dubbed the average American city, and a scale model of the town was later displayed at the 1958 World's Fair in Brussels, Belgium. The area's paper mill had also earned an appellation, "the paper city." Intellectual and religious influences stemmed from the town's numerous colleges and churches.

We had been in Kalamazoo only three weeks when our daughter, Lorna, was born. She put in her appearance on a Sunday morning, a memorable fact in that her arrival wreaked havoc with the usual schedule of services. A blonde little bundle of life, she was as fair as Leon, our second son, was dark. She was endowed with an overall sunny disposition, but behind it was a fiery temperament and an indomitable will. Now, between Leon's two-year-old antics, the demands of the nursery responsibilities for our enlarged family, and the constant parade of guests, which Henry regularly diverted through the parsonage, our house once more became "Grand Central Station."

In many ways, Kalamazoo was a repetition of our Sherwood experience, only on a larger scale. Every Sunday, Henry's increasingly dynamic preaching attracted new listeners, including students from the nearby colleges. Earlier, the church had purchased a site for a new building, and now when Henry proposed a new structure to replace the outmoded and overflowing sanctuary, there was no denying him. The congregation, catching his enthusiasm, rallied to the cause. A building committee was formed. The old property was sold to the Upjohn Company, and ground was broken for the new sanctuary. Henry, clear to all, was a man marked for success.

Life was settling again into a comfortable routine. It had never been so promising for us. But then the shadow began to approach again. First, it hardly seemed to be a shadow at all, but gradually, it began to extend like a long, dark hand, reaching around the circumference of our lives.

The following fall, after we had been in Kalamazoo one year, Henry was troubled by a persistent cough – a mere chest cold, he told himself. At the same time, while driving, he found it difficult to turn the steering wheel with his left arm. A few mornings later as he shaved, he was puzzled because one side of his neck appeared considerably larger than the other. I insisted he see a doctor.

After a cursory exam, the doctor concluded that the problem was a glandular infection. When antibiotics produced no effect, however, the doctor decided to do a biopsy. Though the report was negative, Henry felt strangely apprehensive.

During the winter months, the swelling increased. Lea, now a registered nurse, urged Henry to see a specialist. A month later, Henry visited Dr. Liddig, who, after examining Henry's neck, scheduled him for tests at the nearby Bronson Methodist Hospital. I was told to meet him there.

Stepping outside into the heavenly, gentle snow, I walked up the hill three blocks to the hospital, past the reception desk, onto the elevator, through the nurses' station, to Henry's room. Carefully opening the door, I looked in. There sat Henry, on a chair in a white sheet-like hospital gown. He looked so different without his usual suit and tie, and I said, "You sure look funny in that outfit."

"Valetta, I want you to sit down," he said. "I need to talk to you, and I couldn't wait. I think I'll be out of here soon. Actually, they got the reports back, and I told the doctor to level with me. I wasn't prepared, however, for the results."

I sensed a numbness rising somewhere from the pit of my stomach, that same numbness I had felt listening to Danny's diagnosis. "Valetta," Henry continued, "that little lump on my neck is Hodgkin's disease."

"Hodgkin's?" I echoed. "What's that?"

Henry drew a deep breath. "A type of cancer – cancer of the lymph glands. There may be remissions for a time, but it is fatal. Don't be alarmed, honey, because there is a lot of hope, and God is on our side."

"But," I stammered, "you've never been sick. You can't possibly be sick, not with cancer. You are only twenty-six!"

"We do have time," Henry went on. "We can go on a year, maybe two; we must spend it wisely. Somehow I feel it should be invested for something that will outlast my own life, and I want to talk to you about that."

Prior to that conversation, two events had combined to rivet Henry's attention on foreign missions. First were the dramatic deaths of five young missionaries, martyred for Christ in an attempt to reach a remote tribe of Ecuadorian headhunters, the Aucas, with the Gospel. The second was the coming of Henry's mentor, and my Temperance pastor, Larry Burr, to our area for a missionary rally.

Larry had felt led to leave the pastorate and join a missionary organization, The Oriental Missionary Society (now One Mission Society). With Larry's coming, Henry began to sense the relevance of foreign missions to the local church. As the two men sat talking late one night, Henry expressed his desire to be personally involved in making Christ known beyond the borders of his homeland. Finally he put the question to Larry: "Do you think God might have a place for me in missions?"

"Henry," Larry responded thoughtfully, "if God has put that kind of a desire in your heart, there is no doubt that he is right now preparing you for a future in missionary work. Perhaps, when your work is finished here in Kalamazoo, he will lead you to OMS."

That Sunday night, as Henry had sat on his hospital bed pondering his clouded future, he suddenly felt that he and Larry must talk. Larry had been holding a rally in Vicksburg, a small town a few miles from Kalamazoo. Henry reached him there and said, "Larry, how would you like to preach my funeral sermon?" Larry had known Henry long enough to take this kind of banter without flinching. "Why sure, Henry, any time. You name the place and time, and I'll be there."

"No, Larry, this time I'm serious. I'm in the hospital right now, and the doctors have diagnosed my problem as Hodgkin's disease, cancer of the lymph glands."

There was a long silence. "Look, Henry, I will be right over to see you after this service."

That evening, the two men, who had already shared so much together, talked in subdued voices, as men do when awed with a view of life in an entirely new perspective. "The doctors say I may have no more than a year or two to live and perhaps as little as six months," Henry said. "How do you think I should spend them?"

"Well, Henry," Larry proposed, "if you have the strength, I think you should take a trip to some mission field, preach to those who have never heard, and you will rejoice to see those faces in eternity."

"Pray with me about it, Larry," Henry said. "This may be just what God wants me to do."

With Henry back home, looking and sounding little different from the Henry I had always known, my mind was numb. But now the whole sequence of events had an awful familiarity. We had been through the "countdown" with Danny, and here it was on us again. Somehow, the heart cannot accept what the mind insists is true. I found myself struggling to awaken from a bad dream.

The following Sunday, Henry stood before the congregation. His voice sounded strong and even. Calmly, he announced the results of the hospital tests, concluding, "We can only go ahead and do the work God has given us to do. This is all any of us can do."

The doctors had arranged for Henry to undergo a series of treatments, which hopefully would retard the progress of the disease. The first of these was controlled exposure to X-rays.

When we arrived at the hospital, a group of doctors was waiting. They talked in cold, professional tones and in that mysterious, somehow frightening, medical jargon. Henry was clad in an embarrassingly short hospital gown. He felt uncomfortably conspicuous. He sensed that in their eyes he was just another case history, a diseased organism, an individual without identity. "I have never felt so alone in my whole life," he confided to me.

Carefully, the doctors arranged him on the table under the frighteningly imposing eye of the huge machine. Steel doors closed about him. From his prone position, he could see the doctors looking down on him through the narrow glass of the observation window. There followed an eerie silence, broken suddenly by a deep hum that rose from the heart of the machine, louder and louder. He knew his body was being bombarded by invisible forces that had power to inhibit the growth of the malevolent cells within his body.

The side effects of the treatment were immediate and violent. Though permitted to go home, Henry was frequently seized with a violent nausea, which left him so weak he could hardly climb the stairs to his bedroom. He would ascend a few steps at a time. He was steadily losing weight and was almost never free from a debilitating cough.

Now again, as it happened during the long vigil with Danny, day by day, God opened to me the sweet resources of his Word in special ways. Through the Word, the Holy Spirit can work a curious alchemy, which transmutes pain into comfort and crushing sorrow into sweetness. Romans 8:28, a verse so time worn it has almost become a cliché, was expounded anew to my heart by the Comforter. God would bring good out of this. How? I could not fathom, but he would. I would keep watching for that good. Yes, I would look for miracles, and it would be an adventure.

4

Borne Up Along the
Way of the Cross

B ut, now, what next? The doctors' prognosis, six months,
perhaps a year, drastically altered our perspective on the
future career of Rev. and Mrs. Henry Steel. As we turned to
the Word for guidance, God gave us 1 Peter 4:19: *So if you are
suffering according to God's will, keep on doing what is right
and trust yourself to the God who made you, for he will never
fail you* (TLB).

For the present, at least, we believed that God would have
us carry on in what we were doing. We determined to take
each day as it came, to live in "day-tight compartments," giving ourselves to the things that mattered. It had never been so
easy to sort through the mundane affairs of life and focus on
the "important." As Ben Jonson once said, "The prospect of
immediate death wonderfully concentrates the mind."

"Maybe God wants to heal Henry for his glory," many suggested. We believed in healing and had seen God heal others.
Now, certainly, if anyone had the right to ask for divine healing
as his children, we too had that right. A group of ministers came
and prayed for Henry, anointing him with oil as instructed in

Scripture (James 5:14). After they prayed, Henry began responding to treatments and strength returned.

"Do you feel that God has touched you?" Dale Cryderman asked Henry one day.

"I don't doubt that God has touched me," Henry responded, "but I don't feel that I can say it will be permanent. The doctors say the disease is in remission. Whatever God has for me, though, I pray I'll accept it. My desire is that God will do with my life whatever will bring him the most glory."

Listening to Henry's response, it dawned on me that some deep change was taking place in my husband. There was a quiet poise, yes, a nobility in his sincere, unaffected response that was foreign to the old Henry I had known. God was doing something beautiful in this man, a kind of work of art. Yes, I remembered, *all things work together for good* (Romans 8:28 KJV).

Sensing we needed to get away and be alone to reflect, our people suggested that we take a short vacation to Florida at their expense. Those were blissful days in that picture-postcard setting. We were sweethearts as never before, hand in hand, splashing together in the surf, each experience so sweet, so painfully sweet.

Watching Henry stand tall against the waves and wind, I felt my heart throb with excruciating affection for this courageous man. A cry arose unbidden from my heart, *Oh, Lord, you know how much I love him, how much I need him.* Psalm 90:12 became a kind of theme verse for us at that time. *Teach us to number our days and recognize how few they are; help us to spend them as we should* (TLB).

Back in Kalamazoo, Henry continued to fulfill his responsibilities as pastor, but now, every Sunday, it seemed that he preached with increasing intensity. One morning, looking into the face of the congregation, he spoke fervently, "When we know there are very few tomorrows left, we face some very embarrassing questions. Have I spent too much time finding little answers to little questions? Have I spoken out for Christ only when it was easy to speak for him, repeating the Gospel to those who have heard it hundreds of times while millions have never heard it once? Someday, we tell ourselves, with a little more preparation, experience, and opportunity, then … But suddenly, we realize there will be no more time for preparation, no more experience, no better opportunity. Geographic boundaries and denominational lines vanish, and we see a lost world. No man should live his life presuming on 'tomorrow.' In eternity, there are millions of people who would give everything they have had in this world in order to come back into it for one more day – to do the one thing they had been putting off, right up to the day that they died. No doubt the greatest thing that ever happened to me was to be told by a physician, 'No man can tell you how long it will be.'"

As I listened to Henry's words, I knew he was about to make an announcement that would shake the congregation. For some time he had been in contact with One Mission Society (OMS), the missionary organization with which Larry Burr now served. While attending the OMS annual convention at Winona Lake, Indiana, Henry had shared with their vice president, Bill Gillam, a growing conviction that God was urging him to invest the remaining months of his life in the cause of missions.

When the OMS board met the next week, they did something unprecedented. In view of Henry's unique call and special gifts, they voted to waive the usual health requirements and invited him to join the Society. The plan was that he should take a preliminary trip to South America to better acquaint himself with the work of the mission and then head the regional office in Portland, Oregon.

When the congregation learned of Henry's decision, there was a mixed response. For some, there were tears. People expressed their surprise; some voiced disagreement and questioned the practicality of our choice. After all, was it really wise for a dying man, with perhaps no more than months to live, to leave a secure pastorate and the bosom of a loving congregation?

The next week, a group of key laymen invited Henry to lunch in one of the city's finest restaurants. After a sumptuous meal, a spokesman turned to Henry. "Look at it this way, Pastor," he began, "we want you; we need you. We believe that God still has work for you in Kalamazoo. If your life is cut short by illness, Valetta and the kids will need security, and we can give that to them here." There was a calculated pause while the man waited for his words to register. Then he went on. "We're prepared to make you an offer. If you remain here in Kalamazoo, we will guarantee that your children will be provided for through college. What do you say?"

Later, in addressing a group of missionaries about what it means to cast oneself in faith on God, Henry recalled that moment. "Don't think that it didn't come as a tremendous temptation," he said. "The Devil told me I was a fool to turn down an offer like that. But as I looked into the faces of those generous men with their promises of security, an answer came to me. It wasn't my answer but God's. There is no security, I told them, outside the will of God."

The Hodgkin's disease continued in a state of remission for a full year, far longer than we had dared hope. We saw the new church completed. And now, with each succeeding day of apparently normal life, came a wistful anticipation that possibly the cancer was no longer there. God had heard our cries, we hoped. A miracle had occurred. Henry had been healed. In a short time, we would complete another year at the Kalamazoo church, and Henry would leave on his South American trip, the beginning of service with OMS.

A few days before his departure for South America, however,

came the cruel reminder that Henry was still a dying man. Lying on the bed, mentally reviewing the details of the trip, Henry casually threw his arm across his chest, causing his hand to fall on the back of his neck. What he felt sent a shrill alarm through him. The evil lumps had emerged again. His fingers burned as though the malignant cells were made of fire. For a moment, his spirit faltered.

New X-ray treatments were hastily administered. Henry, armed with a supply of pills, went ahead with the planned tour, but from that time on, indications of the disease appeared with increasing frequency. Painful treatments preceded extensive periods of weakness and gradual recuperation. The short intervals between these treatments marked the relentless march of the malignancy in Henry's body and served as a cruel chronometer, reminding us of his dwindling life expectancy.

Henry's South American tour and our subsequent move to Portland proceeded in spite of our bouts with the disease. Though increasingly frail in health, Henry kept a pace that would have staggered a healthy man. In addition to arranging the itineraries of scores of missionaries, he was in constant demand as a missionary speaker and evangelist at churches and camps throughout the Northwest.

Although Henry avoided mention of his physical condition, his increasing discomfort finally forced him to visit a Christian specialist in Portland who took a personal interest in Henry. Dr. Williams diagnosed his most recent problems as spastic colitis. He was convinced that Henry's system could no longer accept the severe X-ray bombardments, and Henry was forced to begin the alternative and even more excruciating nitrogen mustard gas treatments. Each dose left the patient so violently sick that, for a while, he cared little whether he lived or died. To a visiting friend Henry once confided, "I dread the gas. I dread it with a passion."

With the progression of the disease and a bout with pneu-
monia came increasing lung congestion. From this time on,
he seldom enjoyed a good night's sleep, and he spoke with a
continual wheeze. Every word was an effort. To find relief from
the lung congestion, he would often throw himself face down
across the bed while dictating letters into the Dictaphone on
the floor, and yet there was no thought of stopping.

With the increasingly brief periods of remission, following
the painful mustard gas treatments, Henry would be on the
road again. His now well-known message, *A Dying Man Speaks
to Dying Men*, held congregations transfixed and produced
profound results. Recalling revival services that Henry held at
this time – services in which an entire Mormon family once
came to Christ – a pastor remarked, "Those services were the
most fruitful our church has ever had since its organization."

Each week, as Henry came home and I washed his shirts,
ironed them, and packed them again, I wrestled with a tumult
of conflicting feelings. While I was deeply grateful for the joy
and exhilaration he derived from expending every last ounce
of mortal breath and energy for the sake of his Master, I missed
each moment he was away. I needed him, and his children needed
him. The precious remaining sands of time were pouring so
quickly through the hourglass of his life. So little time remained.

Bob Bletcher, our local pastor, invited Henry for a week of
combined missionary evangelistic services. I was grateful the
meetings were near home where Leon, Lorna, and I could attend.
As I sat there nightly, I detected a new quality in Henry's preaching. He spoke with almost a total lack of self-consciousness.
He seemed to see himself as an embodied illustration of the
Gospel, which proclaims life through death. Somehow, I believe
that in his lonely hours, as he walked the way of the cross with
Christ, he died to Henry Steel. He identified with Christ in a
new way, and he loved to quote Philippians 1:20b-21: *So that*

now as always Christ will be exalted in my body, whether by life or by death. For to me, to live is Christ and to die is gain (NIV).

As he spoke, he would dramatize the sensation of sitting across from the doctor and being told he was a dying man. "But don't feel sorry for me because the doctors say I do not have long to live," he would go on. "There is no difference, really, between you and me, except for maybe a few years. None of us really knows. For all of us, when we stand before Christ, it will not be a matter of how old we are or what age we died, but what we did with Jesus Christ."

One night, I glanced over at Leon as Henry spoke. He sat in the pew beside me as though frozen. His eyes were fixed on his father with remarkable intensity for a seven-year-old. That night, shortly after we had gone to bed, I heard Leon crying. I hurried into his room. "Mommy," he sobbed, "I just saw Jesus dying on the cross in my dreams."

A few weeks later, I took the children with me to Seattle for the closing night of one of Henry's conferences. That evening, he spoke on knowing Christ. After the service, I started to leave the sanctuary with the pastor's wife when I heard a small voice. It was Leon's. "Mom," he said, "can I stay with Dad?"

Sometime later that evening, Henry and Leon walked into the parsonage, smiling. "Valetta," Henry said as we got ready for bed, "this was a very special night for me. Something exciting happened. Leon asked me if he was old enough to become a Christian. You know, I asked the Lord if he would let me lead my son to him before I went to heaven, and tonight he gave me that joy."

When the OMS board convened in Winona Lake in 1962, it made a decision that left me temporarily unhappy and shaken. Impressed with the outstanding work Henry had done in the Northwest, the board asked him to move to mission headquarters in Los Angeles to take charge of all homeland ministries.

"But Henry," I pleaded, "I don't want to move. I'm perfectly happy where we are, and what about your doctor? Who can possibly replace Dr. Williams?"

"Valetta, you may not understand this," Henry soothed, "but I believe God wants me to walk through every open door. I know it doesn't make sense, since there are so many uncertainties about the future, but somehow I'm sure that this is the next step he wants us to take."

In Los Angeles, the famed City of Hope Hospital, outstanding as a cancer research center, admitted Henry as a patient. Henry periodically checked into the City of Hope for the painful treatments required to prolong his dwindling life span. "Well, Valetta," Henry said one day, trying to effect a jaunty joviality I'm sure he didn't feel, "I guess we'll just have to move my office here to the hospital. They want me to check in and stay a little longer this time."

That is what we did. Now, instead of brainstorming in the office, I sat beside his hospital bed while he shared his restless passion to awaken the churches of America to a vision of a world dying without Christ. To the doctors and nurses who knew Henry's condition all too well, but could hardly fathom the burning impulses that drove him on, it must have seemed an aberration of the mind.

Here was a man, as it were, standing on the verge of the grave, yet making plans and dreaming dreams, devising schemes for a future that he would never see. It was irrational, a kind of a madness. One afternoon, while Henry dozed, I strolled up and down the hospital corridors, passing ward after ward of patients, all terminally ill, and Henry was among them. Yes, here was my husband. He too was numbered among the living dead. I began to weep. Tears kept flowing.

As Henry's lungs deteriorated, clogged with growths and scarred by cobalt, each breath became an effort. Nauseated, he found it difficult to keep anything down, and he was put on a special diet. His heart was showing signs of irregularities, side effects of the chemotherapy.

"Lord," I cried one day, "Henry is not getting better, he is getting worse, much worse." At the same time, I could not relinquish hope. After the treatment and nausea would come remission, blessed remission, and with it time, that most precious of all commodities. Once more, Henry responded to treatments: the growths in the lungs began to shrink, and before long he was back home.

Those priceless days, like the last and best perfume in a bottle, Henry determined to pour out upon his Savior. A week after his return home from the hospital, he flew to the OMS Atlanta office to work with Paul and Vi Haines, then on to Indiana where he was keynote speaker at a convention. Following this came consultation with Howard and Wilma Jacob who headed the OMS office at Winona Lake.

"How long do you think Henry will be able to keep up the roadwork?" a missionary colleague asked me. I thought of Christ's words, *Take therefore no thought for the morrow: for the morrow shall take thought for the things of itself. Sufficient unto the day is the evil thereof* (Matt. 6:34 KJV).

"Well," I said, "the Lord doesn't ask us to try to solve tomorrow's problems today." Then I added, "I think Henry will travel just as long as he can." Little did I realize that in the weeks just ahead there would be more traveling for Henry and me than we had ever imagined possible. One long final journey would take him to the very portals of his heavenly home.

A few weeks later, just before Thanksgiving, I received a phone call from Henry. He was still in Indiana. I could sense the excitement in his voice. "Valetta," he said, "how would you like to take a trip with me around the world?"

"You're kidding."

"No, really, someone is writing a blank check for us to take a trip, both of us. They are suggesting we go to Europe, to the Holy Land, wherever we wish. I feel maybe God wants us to visit the OMS fields in Asia and Greece."

"But, Henry," I sputtered, "what about the children, and who will run things at the office?"

"I know," he answered, "and of course you are wondering about my health. Frankly, so am I. Valetta, why don't you make a list of all the obstacles, and let's pray about each one specifically."

"Henry, you know I'd be thrilled to go if, if ..."

"Valetta," he put in, "let's just trust God for some miracles."

Les Ike, our mission treasurer, and his wife, Pat, offered to take care of Leon in our absence, and our dear friend, Flo Rickards, who worked in our Men for Missions office, insisted that she stay with Lorna. One more hurdle remained. Henry knew he dare not make a trip without the approval of his doctors at the City of Hope.

"You're a very sick man," the doctors agreed, "but if problems develop, you can always fly home. We see no real danger in your going."

OMS leaders agreed reluctantly. "We feel hesitant about letting you make such a strenuous trip in your condition," they explained. "It hardly seems wise, and yet if God is leading you, who are we to say no?"

It seemed that God had removed every obstacle. We called a missions travel agent, Howard Hill, and asked him to write out our tickets. Our itinerary would take us to Greece, India, Japan, Korea, Hong Kong, Taiwan, Hawaii, and back to Los Angeles.

We left New York in a snowstorm, and by the time we reached Athens, the first stopover on our itinerary, it was clear to me that Henry was experiencing increasing discomfort. His persistent cough was worse. He was running a high fever and felt nauseated. When OMS missionaries met us at the airport, we agreed that Henry should be under a doctor's care. A doctor soon admitted him to a Greek hospital.

I was assailed by doubts and was on the verge of despair. Had we been out of our minds to think of attempting an around-the-world trip with Henry so desperately sick? Possibly he was dying in this unfamiliar environment, and we were trying to communicate with medical personnel who knew little English. It was an experience that filled me with uneasiness, bordering on feelings of terror. Armed with a Greek-English dictionary, I shopped little markets at night, hunting for snacks that Henry might like.

Two days after chemotherapy, Henry again revived, almost miraculously it seemed. We boarded the plane for the next leg of our journey. In India, we were met by OMS field director Wesley Duewel, who would soon be elected Mission president.

We visited the city of Benares – holy to Hindus – on the banks of the famous Ganges River. Mingling with masses of staggering humanity, we watched Hindu pilgrims trying to wash away their sins in the polluted waters. We toured ornate Hindu temples and were shocked by scenes of sexual perversion, depicted in shameless detail on the walls.

On a trip to the villages, I came down with a fever. As I dragged myself along, I looked at Henry, stooped with pain. Here we were, two invalids, surrounded by a dismal procession of human beings – impoverished, sad, homeless, blind – shuffling along beside us. It seemed as if the whole world were sick.

We visited one of the churches and listened to our Christian brothers singing their *budjins*, the hauntingly beautiful ethnic music of the Indian people. Wesley told us of believers standing heroically for Christ in the face of ostracism and persecution from Hindu relatives and neighbors. Our time in India left us with hearts freshly wounded for a world without Christ. I later established a memorial fund in Henry's name for the building of churches in India. I knew he would have wanted that.

From India, we flew to Hong Kong, that crowded crossroads of the Orient, then on to Korea to see OMS's largest work. At the airport, our missionaries Ed and Elmer Kilbourne, along with dozens of Korean believers, greeted us. "We have prayed you around the world on your journey to heaven," they said. "We believe God is going to visit us through you."

Henry's pain was increasing. Besieged with fits of coughing and nausea, he could sleep for only brief periods. Doctors urged that he be admitted to a hospital, but he would not hear of it. Henry was scheduled to preach each evening to the more than 500 pastors who had gathered for the churches' annual conference. This is what he had come to Korea for, and he would do it even if he died in the pulpit. He did it, sometimes gasping and heaving, but he was sustained somehow through the delivery of each sermon. Those who heard the messages, the last that Henry ever preached from a pulpit, will never forget them.

During the long sleepless nights as Henry struggled for breath, I cast myself upon the Lord in prayer and poured over precious passages of Scripture for courage and comfort. One evening, God's presence enveloped me with an overwhelming sweetness. The Holy Spirit seemed to direct me to Isaiah 58:8: *Then shall thy light break forth as the morning, and thine health shall spring forth speedily: and thy righteousness shall go before thee; the glory of the LORD shall be thy reward* (KJV).

"Lord," I asked, "is this word for Henry? Are you going to heal him right here in Korea?" The next night I was drawn to the same chapter. "Lord," I said, "what does this mean? Do you want me to accept a different kind of healing from what I would desire?"

"Soon," the Holy Spirit whispered to me, "soon Henry's healing will be total and eternal."

From Korea we went on to Taiwan, where we were met by OMS field director Rolland Rice. Missionaries gathered in the Rices' living room while Henry, reclining on the sofa, talked to them. Hunched over now and in continual pain, he still managed to visit the churches and to take a trip to beautiful Sun Moon Lake. The final leg of our flight took us to Hawaii for a brief stopover and then on home to Los Angeles.

Sunday and Monday we reserved for Leon and Lorna and a few close friends. These quiet hours together were filled with hugs and kisses and stories about our trip.

The next evening, I packed Henry's bag and prepared for the leisurely drive to the City of Hope where the doctors were expecting him. As we went out the door, Lorna looked at Henry accusingly.

"Daddy, why are you always sick?" she demanded.

"Sweetie," he answered, "Daddy has been sick since you were a baby, but you must thank Jesus that he has let your daddy live long enough so that you will be able to remember him." Leon looked on silently, his big eyes wistful and sad.

The following day, Henry's lungs became so congested that he was placed in an oxygen tent. The next two days he rested almost continuously. On the fourth day, doctors told me Henry was on the critical list. I stayed through the night, praying there would be yet another remission.

I listened to the oxygen equipment, pumping away, and Henry's labored breathing in rhythm with the machine. Like some kind of mechanical octopus, the machine seemed as if it were reaching out and seizing my husband's body. I was losing him. Late in the evening, I left the hospital to drive home for a few hours of rest. As I followed the stream of red taillights, I found myself thinking of the funeral. What kind of funeral would Henry want?

I had been home only a few hours when the phone rang. I

picked it up. The voice on the other end was cold, impersonal. "I have sad news for you, Mrs. Steel," the doctor began. Just seven days after arriving home from our world trip, Henry had embarked on a new journey to a better place.

He had wanted to be buried in the Sherwood Cemetery in a small plot of ground where we had laid our firstborn, Danny, to rest. The funeral would be held in the new sanctuary of the Kalamazoo church, which stood as a monument to the vision God had given Henry. On May 5, Leon, Lorna, and I, accompanied by OMS President Dr. Eugene Erny, boarded a flight from Los Angeles to Chicago. When our plane touched down at O'Hare International Airport, friends were on hand to meet us and escort us to Kalamazoo.

As the funeral service began, I took my place at the front of the church. Beside me sat Lorna, minus her two front teeth, a normal six year old, and beside her sat Leon, dark and tall for his eight years. My thoughts wandered back over my life with Henry – our first meeting on the campus of Spring Arbor College, our growing friendship, working together on the yearbook and school paper, the chime of wedding bells, our first pastorate in the quiet little town of Sherwood, the building of this lovely church, and the miracle years in missions. A whole chapter of my life was ending like the final pages of a book.

That afternoon, I felt God take my hand in a way that was almost more literal than figurative. His Spirit reached out to embrace me through a host of loving people: family ministers, missionaries, friends from Sherwood and Kalamazoo. Suddenly, in my mind's eye, I had a vision of my husband, now in his resurrected body, triumphant, no longer burdened with pain, running eagerly to meet his Lord. With outstretched arms, Jesus was saying to him, *Well done, thou good and faithful servant* (Matthew 25:21 KJV). Frank Gorsline, a lad whom Henry had led to Christ years before in Sherwood, now under appointment as a missionary to Brazil, stood to sing a song that so aptly summed up the spirit of Henry Steel:

> The path that I have trod,
>   Has brought me nearer God,
> Though often led through sorrow's gate,
>   Though not the way I choose,
> In my way I might lose
>   The joy that yet for me awaits.
>
> Not what I wish to be,
>   Nor where I wish to go,
> For who am I that I should choose my way.
>   The Lord shall choose for me,
> 'Tis better far I know,
>   So let him bid me go or stay.

After the funeral, Dad approached me. "Valetta," he said, "we have a place for you in our business, and a house is waiting. You know we would love to have you back in Temperance."

"I'll think about it," I responded, but deep within myself I knew my mind was already made up. Henry's call had been my call. God had led us out of the pastorate to invest our lives in missions, and though Henry's task was completed, I did not feel as if I had been released from God's call. The trip to Asia had only deepened my burden for missions and the millions beyond our borders who were without Christ. Moreover, I had found an identity of spirit and an extended family among OMS missionaries. The Mission had asked me to continue to work at headquarters. I knew my answer would be yes.

As we left the church that afternoon, Leon turned to me and solemnly observed, "You know, Mom, this is a great day for Dad, but a sad one for us."

I blinked back the tears. His profound words found a painful echo in my heart. Henry's life had been heroic. I could look back over it without a moment's regret. But now the future yawned before me like a vast dark chasm. How could I walk that valley alone? Could I be the kind of parent I ought to be? Without Henry, it all seemed impossible.

5

A Discovery of Identity
Through Sorrow

I was walking the valley the second time. The first time, when Danny died, I had Henry to lean upon. He had been my tower of strength, the one human being I instinctively turned to for comfort and counsel, the one I had clung to when the billows of life threatened to overwhelm me. But now it was different. Henry was gone, out of my earthly life forever. I ached for human arms to hold me in my sorrow, human hands to wipe away my tears.

As the full significance of Henry's death settled down on me, at first it was as though I were caught in a vacuum, or as though all the clocks in the world had suddenly stopped. Time was standing still. I felt engulfed in an interminable aching void.

The day after I returned to Los Angeles from the funeral, I got up as usual, sent the kids off to school, and then walked across the street to the OMS headquarters building where I had my office. I entered through the same doors and passed the same familiar desks and faces, but it was not the same. The landscape of my life had now changed irrevocably.

I sat down to read the mail and glanced over at Henry's empty chair – one of many he would never sit in again. I noticed a stack of letters on his desk – letters he would never answer. Suddenly, wave upon wave of grief swept over me. *Lord,* I prayed, *I need a miracle just to get through this day.*

And always, there was the house to go back to. We had not lived there long, but already it had become home. Every room was tenderly haunted with the ghost of Henry. The halls still echoed with recent conversations, laughter, sighs.

I went out to the garage and noticed Henry's books, stacked neatly in boxes against a wall. We had been so busy since coming from Portland, he had not even had time to unpack them. There was his deer rifle, a new Kodak camera, his mounted deer antlers from Montana, and hundreds of colored slides from our travels across the United States.

That was about it, though. Henry didn't leave many material things, I comforted myself, but he left something infinitely more valuable – an example of a heroic kind of love for his Master. It was a legacy that I would repeatedly draw inspiration from in the months and years ahead.

What should I do with Henry's belongings? His clothing still hung in the closet, his shoes were on the floor, and personal objects were scattered about the room. I decided that, for the time being, I would leave his things just as they were. Later, when I had come to terms with my grief, I would sort through them, give some of them away, and keep others for the children, but not yet.

I was not ready to bear the wrenching act of parting with those memory-laden accoutrements of my husband's mortal life. I have heard that the Jews have a special time for mourning, a time when the bereaved focuses on his grief and weeps. It is a time for release and cleansing without guilt, a natural expression of human sorrow. I think this is wise, and I feel God approves. Leon and Lorna saw my tears and shared them.

At times I would gather them in my arms, and the three of us would talk of Henry and weep together.

Though I continued working in the same office, I perceived that my role had changed. For years, I had worked as my husband's associate, but now I was passed over in much of the planning and brainstorming sessions I so relished.

I felt like a drudge, a misfit. I was routinely pounding out letters on a typewriter. I lived in a man's world, it seemed. *Only men share ideas in this office,* I thought. A woman? What could she contribute? I had ideas, plenty of them, but I had never learned how to sell them. Henry had always done that for me. The administration had listened to him. He was very articulate, and he was a man. *Lord,* I cried inwardly, *help me find out where I belong.*

For the first time in my life, I was introduced to loneliness. Often in the past, trying to match my husband's frantic pace, I yearned for a patch of solitude. But now I was experiencing a kind of stark loneliness I never really knew existed before. I longed for adult companionship. On weekends, when couples got together for outings or evenings of fellowship, I often felt disregarded.

At home, having once prided myself on being in control of things, I found it increasingly difficult to cope. One afternoon, Tammy, our big German shepherd, jumped through the screen and began running away. At the same moment, Leon and Lorna came in the back door. Their relationship, which, at best, seemed an uneasy truce, had suddenly given way to violence. "Mommy," Lorna screamed, "Leon is hitting me."

Those kids are fighting all the time, I thought to myself. *How will I ever get them to care for each other?* We had to find the dog. There was dinner to fix, and I didn't feel hungry. "Lord, where can you find good in all of this?" I demanded.

The routines of life called for decisions, always decisions, but

I had lost confidence in my ability to make even the simplest decisions. Being decisive required mental energy, and I had no energy to draw from. I was weary. It was an effort just to arrange my jumbled thoughts long enough to solve the most mundane problems. I went through the day's schedule like a robot.

What, Lord, has happened to my joy, my enthusiasm, my motivation? I cried out. In the same friendly office, the friendliest face was missing. By contrast, everything seemed cold and lifeless. The little house, where friends used to gather for boisterous, fun-filled evenings, now seemed empty and bare. *If only,* I thought, *Henry could once again walk in that door.* But Henry would never again do that. The thought unleashed waves of depression and self-pity.

The world around me had turned into a featureless plain. People I passed on the streets had no faces; I hardly saw them. Driving over the familiar concrete stretches of the Los Angeles freeway, crowded with automobiles, I felt more isolated than on the country farm where I grew up. On one particular day, absorbed in the tangle of my own thoughts, I missed my turn-offs, suddenly discovering that I did not know where I was, not even sure how to get back home. It seemed somehow symbolic. My life had become like that – a long dull stretch of road that I was traveling, hardly knowing where I was going or where to get off.

I have shared all of this as frankly as I know how to underscore a plain truth: Christians are in no way exempt from the tragedies of life. We share in the curses and frailties of that nature common to all men. Death, that savage intruder, has the power to break our hearts, to leave us demoralized, and for a time, under the tyranny of despair.

And yet, when the worst that can happen has indeed happened, when the heart is broken, the tears have flowed, and unanswered questions have been wrung in anguish from the soul – a discovery comes. To some it comes sooner, and to some, later.

The discovery is simple: God has not left his children without resources.

I had known the comfort of his Word when I cradled my dying son in the little Sherwood parsonage, through the night hours when I tried to quench his unquenchable thirst. Yes, God had spoken then. I had known it in the guest room in Korea as I listened to my husband struggling to draw breath into his tormented lungs; God had spoken both times, and my heart had been at peace. Now he was gently instructing again.

To my surprise and delight, I discovered the Scriptures did indeed bring healing for my latest grief. Every cliché that I had ever heard about his Word was true, really true. It was light in the darkness, bread to the hungry, a staff to the weak, water for parched lips. *"The words that I speak unto you,"* Jesus said, *"they are spirit, and they are life"* (John 6:63 KJV). How true.

I learned, as Amy Carmichael expressed it, to find "gold by moonlight." I started a special notebook in which I stored up my treasures. Many of these verses, long familiar mottos, were now peculiarly apt, as though the Holy Spirit was fitting them like a skillful tailor to every dimension of my life: *Weeping may endure for a night, but joy cometh in the morning* (Psalm 30:5 KJV). *Since the Lord is directing our steps, why try to understand everything that happens along the way?* (Proverbs 20:24 TLB). *For it is God who works in you to will and to act according to his good purpose* (Philippians 2:13 NIV). *We can make our plans, but the final outcome is in God's hands* (Proverbs 16:1 TLB). *Commit your work to the Lord, then it will succeed* (Proverbs 16:3 TLB). *We should make plans – counting on God to direct us* (Proverbs 16:9 TLB). *The Lord destroys the possessions of the proud but cares for widows* (Proverbs 15:25 TLB).

Like the psalmist, I had discovered that God's rod and

staff – his Word – were indeed my comfort in the valley of the shadow of death (Psalm 23:4). And like the shepherd's instrument, God used his rod not only for comfort and safety, but also for guidance and correction. God knew there were faulty areas in my life that needed correction. Lovingly, he brought the chastening rod of his Word to bear on those deficiencies.

The first problem that God began to deal with me about was in the area of self-worth. Henry's passing had devastated that part of me. His death left me groping for some kind of identity. Unconsciously, I had come to see myself as an adjunct to my dynamic and successful husband. I identified with his achievements, realizing my own contributions to them, and basked in the approval that he drew from his colleagues. His ministry gave me opportunities and brought me fulfillment. Now, in a moment, that comfortable role had vanished. I was stripped of my husband and my self-esteem. I was Valetta, alone, no longer Mrs. Steel. Who was I, really? What was I worth?

I looked at myself in the mirror. At thirty, I was not very old, but I saw wrinkles. I had experienced a lot of life, and my experience made me cautious. Invitations to go places and try new things that would have been met with enthusiasm ten years earlier were now greeted with hesitancy and the turmoil of inner questions.

I realized that mentally I was keeping a record book in which I assessed my strengths and weaknesses; it was a kind of ledger. What I was convinced were my true strengths, I listed in the credit column. My weaknesses – areas in which I had experienced feelings of inadequacy and failure – I put in the debit column.

I recalled one disastrous attempt I had made in trying to teach Sunday school. What agony I endured as I tried to ignite a spark of interest while my little students, completely unappreciative of my efforts, proceeded to wiggle and talk. I had come away from that experience with the attitude that I would limit my activities to the safe and comfortable ruts in which I felt secure. I would diligently avoid service opportunities that I perceived to be threatening. I would pride myself on being humble enough to acknowledge my limitations. But was that the way God wanted me to live?

No! And the word he gave me on this subject was John 6:63: *It is the spirit that quickeneth; the flesh profiteth nothing* (KJV). It was time, the Holy Spirit seemed to say, to quit mulling over the dreary catalog of my failures, time to commit those failures to God, acknowledging that apart from God, the flesh is worthless. Even the great successes of the flesh are often negative factors creating rampant pride and rendering us unusable to the Lord. I needed to start trusting the Holy Spirit to bring strength out of my weaknesses.

Coupled with John 6:63, I felt the Holy Spirit urging me on to another verse that I had so glibly quoted in easier times, Philippians 4:13: *I can do all things through Christ which strengtheneth me* (KJV). My heart really leaped when I grasped that principle. I am nothing, a big zero, in myself, but Jesus is living in me. His presence in me gives me self-worth. He wants to live out his life in me, enabling me to bring glory to God.

Other verses that helped underscore this truth, which God was using to change the tenor of my life and the direction of my ministry, were 2 Corinthians 12:9: *I am with you; that is all you need. My power shows up best in weak people* (TLB); and 2 Corinthians 4:7: *But this precious treasure—this light and power that now shine within us—is held in a perishable container, that is, in our weak bodies. Everyone can see that the glorious power within must be from God and is not our own* (TLB).

Still there was another hurdle. I am a woman, and my view of womankind had unconsciously been shaped to a great extent by my culture and family. Almost every daughter's role model is her mother. My mother had passed on to me many strengths: loyalty, responsibility, honesty, and modesty, for instance. However, she had always been one to linger in the background, relinquishing the role of spiritual leader to Dad. With Henry, who was the prototype of the aggressive, self-confident leader, I too had been content to fade into the background. That was the woman's place I had come to accept – behind the scenes, expediently meek and obscure.

Now, as I studied the New Testament, God began to speak to me about my warped view of the woman's role. I believe the Gospel has always liberated women. I began to notice that women played a vital part in the spread of early Christianity. On Paul's missionary journeys, the Gospel first took root in the hearts of devoted women. Lydia was the key layperson in the founding of the Philippian church (Acts 16:11-15). Many of Paul's coworkers in missionary enterprises were women. Is it not significant that in the Scriptures, contrary to Eastern protocol, Priscilla appears before her husband Aquila (Romans 16:3)? As a teacher of doctrine, she was possibly more gifted and prominent than her husband. She did not hesitate to exhort and instruct the eloquent evangelist Apollos.

During this time, God helped me find acceptance in another problem area – singleness. With Henry gone, I had joined that swelling segment of society that we have branded "singles." We lump together in this category those who seem to be life's misfits – individuals who have never landed a mate, those whose marriages have come apart, as well as widows and widowers who have been "reduced" to single status by the intervention of premature and untimely death of spouses. The penalty for being single meant exclusion from family-oriented events, a dearth of adult companionship, and long, lonely evenings made even lonelier for want of intimate conversation with a mate.

Were single people really second rate? How did God regard

them? Again the Holy Spirit spoke to me through the Word. I read 1 Corinthians 7:17: *But be sure in deciding these matters that you are living as God intended, marrying or not marrying in accordance with God's direction and help, and accepting whatever situation God has put you into* (TLB). And 1 Corinthians 7:7: *But we are not all the same. God gives some the gift of a husband or wife, and others he gives the gift of being able to stay happily unmarried* (TLB).

In my study of the Gospel narratives, I was impressed that Jesus had given of himself to people regardless of their economic or social status. He saw them only as individuals, whether rich, poor, educated, illiterate, married, or single. I determined that I would address people in the same way – as individuals created in God's image. I would recognize what God was doing in their lives. How could I help?

Once I lost my self-consciousness about being single, I began to feel equally comfortable with families, couples, or other singles. It simply did not matter anymore. I was sure that I was living as Paul had said, *In accordance with God's direction*, and for the present, that meant being single. There was dignity and honor in that.

Finally, during this period, when God was taking the twisted remnants of my life and reshaping them into a new design, he began to deal with me about my faulty understanding of happiness. God rebuked me first through the lips of my son, Leon.

"Mom," Leon bluntly asked me one day, "why do you always look so unhappy?"

It was true, devastatingly true, that the joy had seeped out of my life, and I complained to the Lord. *Nothing is turning out as I had planned. Why, Lord? Why did you take away my happiness?*

God began to show me his answers to the problem of my

misery. The verse he used was James 4:3: *Ye ask, and receive not, because ye ask amiss* (KJV).

But Lord, I protested, *I'm just asking you for happiness. What's wrong with that? How is that asking amiss? You want me to be happy, don't you? Your Word is full of talk about how Christians should be happy.*

Yes, my child, he seemed to answer. *I want you to be happy, overflowing with irrepressible joy, but that joy is only a by-product. It comes when you seek something else.*

What, Lord?

My will, Valetta, my will.

Now I came to verse 10 of James 4: *Humble yourselves in the sight of the LORD, and he shall lift you up* (KJV). That verse had my name on it. *Lord,* I prayed, *please forgive my self-pity and self-centered life. All I think about are my problems. Please change me, and help me to live for you.* Then I added, *Lord, I totally relinquish to you my ideas of what I think life should be, and I ask you to give me your ideas.*

My prayers began to change. As I tried each day to make pleasing God the goal of my life, it occurred to me that since Jesus came to save lost, despairing people, it would please him if I would spend time reaching out to those same people, telling them about his life, death, and resurrection.

I realized with a jolt that doing this would indeed be "witnessing." I had heard that word thundered from my husband's pulpit. It was what every Christian should do, must do, to show that he or she was spiritual. Witness. That meant going out into public places, collaring people, warning them of hell and judgment, urging them to repent. Witness. The word evoked both guilt and fear in me. That seemed strange because telling others about Jesus was witnessing, and that was what God wanted me to do.

As soon as I felt ready to concentrate my life's focus on

ministry, God brought into my life the exact person I needed to meet. Her name was Kathy Rice, now Mrs. Bruce Narramore, and she was on the staff of Campus Crusade for Christ.

Kathy, it seemed, was everything I was not. She was friendly, outgoing, and, above all, self-confident. Where she had strengths, I had nothing but weaknesses. But God had already made himself clear on that subject; the whole point of what he was doing in me was to perfect his power through my weakness.

"Kathy," I asked timidly, "would you mind going with me to the park down the street and letting me watch as you share your faith with someone?"

"Wow, I would love that, Valetta," Kathy said enthusiastically. "Now, what we wear is important," she explained. "Let's dress casually. We don't want to appear too different. People might think we have problems, not answers."

Astonished, I watched Kathy share her faith with a young mother. Her approach was neither preachy nor intimidatingly know-it-all. After some small talk, Kathy casually had said, "May I share something with you that has helped me a lot and see if it makes sense to you?"

"Well, sure," came the reply, "why not?"

Can witnessing really be that simple? I asked myself.

The next Sunday, I noticed an attractive Spanish-American lady who looked about my age and had slipped into the back of our Sunday school class. The Holy Spirit nudged me, and after class, I greeted the woman. Nervously and with reserve, I tried to remember how Kathy would have begun. But then I began to feel a powerful love rising from deep within me and reaching out to this woman.

"Have you ever had the wonderful experience of knowing God in a personal way?" I blurted out.

She looked at me intently. "You know," she said, "I've been trying to find God in a personal way for a long, long time."

Excited, I opened my Bible and began to explain God's simple plan of salvation. When I invited her to pray a sinner's prayer, she responded with joy. We became friends.

God's promise was being fulfilled in a way that exceeded all my expectations. As I tried to please him, not myself, my life brimmed with a happiness and exuberance that I had not known before.

God began regularly to point out specific individuals with whom he wanted me to share his Good News. I once made an appointment to witness to a relative and discovered another heart already prepared.

A few doors down from me lived a professional woman. The clothes she wore and the tilt of her head suggested a worldly-wise self-assurance. She was a Hollywood photographer. I had been told she was an atheist. Inviting her over one day, we made small talk over coffee.

Summoning my courage, I said, "I've made a discovery that has helped me a lot, and since you are obviously an intelligent person, I wonder if you would listen and see if it makes sense to you."

"Of course," she responded, "please share your discovery with me."

I did, and she did not agree with all I said. She objected vigorously to some of it, but when she left, we were friends. The seed had been planted, and God would water it, I trusted.

I received an invitation to speak at a women's retreat, and other invitations followed. With the help of a journalist friend from Portland, I put together a slide presentation with taped narration and background music; it dramatized the sadness of people who live and die without the opportunity of once hearing of Christ. Incredible as it seemed, God was using me, Valetta Steel. In dying to my own pursuit of happiness, I had discovered the true source of joy.

6

A Widow's Seeds of Vision

In January 1966, I left Los Angeles. My car was part of a caravan, an odd assortment of vehicles moving like a giant caterpillar toward the new OMS World Headquarters in Greenwood, Indiana, a thriving suburb of Indianapolis. In 1921, mission founders Charles and Lettie Cowman had located in southern California in the hope that Mr. Cowman, a dying man, would benefit from the mild climate. Since the bulk of OMS constituency had for many years been concentrated in the Midwest, the move back to Indiana was unquestionably sound strategy. It situated the mission command center close to supporting churches and key institutions.

In Greenwood, I moved into mission housing across the street from headquarters. I soon found a warm welcome in a thriving downtown church pastored by a dynamic young minister, Don Riggs. When neighborhood youth stopped by my home, I began to put into practice the principles God had given me for reaching out to confused and hurting young people. On Sundays, we would load the kids into a car and take them to hear Don preach.

"Look, Valetta," Pastor Riggs said to me one day. "I've

noticed that everywhere you go you've got young people with you. I think God has given you a gift of relating to youth. How about taking over our college and career Sunday school class?"

I caught my breath as I felt the old fears of inadequacy surging back over me. Satan brought to mind a vivid rerun of my earlier Sunday school teaching fiasco, reminding me that I had so firmly concluded that I was not cut out to be a teacher. As I paused, groping for words, the One who *hath not given us the spirit of fear* (2 Timothy 1:7 KJV) reminded me that taking my weaknesses and turning them into his strengths is what the Christian life is about. "Forgive me, Lord," I whispered. And then in a voice that I hoped sounded full of confidence and enthusiasm, I said, "Sure, Don, I'd be thrilled to take the class."

Sunday mornings presented me with a challenge I had never experienced before. I recalled the scores of times I had sat in Sunday school class, bored, because there was little opportunity for participation. It was my hope that every student would become a teacher and that each one would feel responsible for sharing spiritual insights. Since the teacher usually learns more than the students, I wanted to find ways to help each class member share in leadership. I began with polls of their current interest topics.

Could I risk a new teaching approach? Believing I should try, I chose eight people to lead discussion groups – approximately half the class – and my main responsibility was to guide the student leaders. It was then that the class doubled and finally tripled. I discovered the Holy Spirit is the dynamic Teacher.

Exhausted and excited, I was discovering a spiritual principle that was new for me. Whatever investment I made in these lives was being returned manyfold. Every week, I met young people with eager hearts and questioning minds – medical students, a lawyer, nurses, lab technicians, clerks, secretaries. Each life

I touched left me somehow enriched and changed. God was taking a timid widow and stretching and enlarging her.

My sister Lea Ullom and her husband, Virgil, were living on the campus of Indiana University, where Virgil was studying dentistry. When I dropped in on them periodically, God opened doors for more contact with Indiana University (IU) students. Their home became an informal student fellowship center.

My class at the church continued to grow as members became involved in leadership and brought their friends, many from broken homes and a few on drugs. One young man, Joey, was really spaced out. His lifeless, vacant stare bore witness to the debilitating effect of drugs. In time, I watched with growing excitement as the Word of God penetrated the fog of Joey's mind. He became a discussion leader eventually.

My neighbor, Judy Ike, once brought a friend, George, who was a football player at the local high school. When George trusted Christ as Savior, he was so eager to share his newfound faith that he became one of my teaching assistants.

Rick, recently returned from Vietnam, was broken, guilt-ridden, and demoralized by drugs; he soon joined our class. The class witnessed high drama as God's power rebuilt his shattered life, vividly illustrating 2 Corinthians 5:17: *Therefore, if anyone is in Christ, he is a new creation; the old has gone, the new has come!* (NIV). Leon soon discovered he had acquired a big brother in Rick – an added blessing from God.

Another young man, Steve, was a psychology major and a bit of a skeptic. Steve had gone to Sunday school as a child, but by the time he joined my class, he had concluded that the Bible was "hardly relevant" to the needs of modern man. And yet, he found himself trying to account for the profound effects the Word was having on the lives of people like Rick and Joey. He was doing some deep thinking; he dusted off his Bible and began reading it again.

One afternoon he called me on the phone. "Valetta, I see it so clearly," he began, his voice trembling with emotion. "I have been reading James, and what he said two thousand years ago about so many things seems so relevant today."

In a flash, Steve had seen in James 1:22-25 that real learning takes place not merely through reason and introspection – mental processes – but by applying truth, living it out in human life. This insight became a driving force for Steve and his wife, Sharon, as they shared Christ with friends and became class discussion leaders.

Steve insisted that so many people were studying the Bible, but that they were not really learning because they hadn't learned to apply the principles. Faith grows only as it is used, he would say. As their vision broadened, Steve and Sharon began a ministry of prison evangelism. Then they started a program to teach high school students in the church to share their faith. The students included Leon and Lorna.

Meanwhile, at OMS headquarters, I worked for the vice president of home ministries, Merv Heebner. My job consisted of typing, filing, answering the phone, writing, and assisting in various programs – all indispensable services. I saw the importance of OMS, a Christian organization with more than three hundred missionaries on thirteen fields in Asia, Latin America, and Europe.

Certainly this was an important ministry I had been performing, I assured myself. And yet I sensed a growing restlessness, as though God was again nudging me. *What does this mean, Lord?* I asked. *Is this restlessness simply my human impatience? If you want me to continue in the office routine, I am content to do that for your glory; but Lord, if you have something more, I am willing, and I am listening.*

With a vacation coming up, I had planned a two-week tour of our OMS field in Haiti, a forlorn, corruption-ridden republic six hundred miles from the coast of Florida with the lowest per capita income of any country in the world. Accompanying me would be my sister Lea and her husband, Virgil, soon to be graduated from dental school, and a young doctor, Esther Schubert, who was completing her medical training at IU. All three were seeking God's place for their future service. The brief trip was destined to dramatically alter each of our lives in different ways. In Haiti, Esther would meet her future husband; Lea and Virgil would discover God's place for them, and I would find a new calling.

The moment we disembarked from our comfortable womb of a Pan American jet, we were plunged into an environment so shockingly different, we might as well have been in the heart of Africa rather than ninety minutes from Miami. We threaded our way through the streets, crowded with small vehicles, animals, and people. We were jostled by dark bodies, and small hands were thrust at us. "Five cents, missus. This way, missus," I heard.

Aboard the mission van, we bumped along over a rutted highway that snaked through rugged mountains shrouded with mist and through dilapidated villages and collections of mud huts covered with straw or corrugated tin roofs. Forlorn women prepared scraps of food over open fires, while naked children with bloated bellies played in the dirt.

Our old rattletrap vehicle carried us past fields of sugar cane and forests of mahogany trees, eventually taking us to the center of OMS work on the island. Here were some substantial concrete buildings, radio studios, missionary homes, a clinic, a church, and a school.

The following day, Mardy Picazo, one of the missionaries who had pioneered the Haiti work, showed us through the Emmaus Vocational Bible School. We observed bright-faced, alert young people learning basic agricultural and industrial skills along with the Scriptures. "These young people have found Christ in our churches," Mardy explained. "Most of their families live in mud houses or grass huts."

Beyond the Bible school, we came to the OMS-related Bethesda Medical Clinic where we saw long lines of people patiently waiting for medical attention. One mother had brought a small baby who was nearly dead from malnutrition. As nurses fed the listless infant with a dropper, the mother hungrily licked the milk that dribbled down her baby's chin. We saw missionaries working side by side with trained Haitians, administering doses of compassion and comfort along with medicine. Periodically a pastor and a nurse joined in prayer for these Haitians or invoked the power of Jesus' name for deliverance from evil spirits.

On Sunday morning, we made our way down a narrow dirt path to a "brush arbor" church. We found that these simple wooden structures, covered with branches, served as temporary churches until more permanent structures could be built. As we took our seats on the narrow boards that served as benches, the Haitian pastor led the congregation in a hymn. Voiced in swelling, rhythmical Creole, the radiant, mahogany-colored countenances contrasted darkly with the sad, gaunt faces of the voodoo-haunted people we had seen in the market places.

The Haiti experience was crucial in all of our lives. By the time our two weeks were up and we boarded the plane for the return trip to Indianapolis, Virgil and Lea had offered their lives to God in service to the Haitian people. Virgil visualized the establishment of a dental clinic – a dream that would one day be beautifully realized.

But in the meantime, before Virgil had his diploma and he and Lea had left Indiana University, was there not something God wanted them to do? IU was not Haiti, but it certainly was a "place to witness." All around them, students faced emotional and spiritual problems, and many marriages were disintegrating.

All of us felt burdened for this college community, and I began to wonder how God wanted to use us there.

I had recently read an article in a *Moody Monthly* magazine that described how Christian women had been inviting neighbors over for coffee and then proceeding to share Christ with them. Sometimes an outstanding professional woman with whom these housewives could identify would give her witness. The neighborhood coffees had proven remarkably effective in reaching women for Jesus Christ.

Would a coffee work in an academic community? I wondered. There was only one way to find out. Virgil, Lea, and I set a date, secured a room on campus, and sent out one hundred invitations.

Only four people responded, indicating they were interested in coming, and all were Christians. Our noble project turned out to be one gigantic washout, and we canceled the event. As we sat commiserating, it dawned on me that God was bringing something good out of this. To begin with, we had acquired four new friends, and as we shared our burden with them, they all expressed a desire to be a part of our team.

Furthermore, we discovered that we had made three strategic errors. We had not checked the campus calendar and had inadvertently scheduled our coffee on the night of the big dance. Second, we had not delivered invitations personally and thus decided that next time, all invitations would be delivered face to face or by phone. Finally, it occurred to us that the genius of the women's coffees lay partly in the fact that they were held in homes, not in intimidating church buildings or public halls. We determined, therefore, to seek a casual atmosphere where it would be natural and easy to open up and talk about one's faith.

Immediately we set about planning another coffee. Lea and I and our new friends met to pray for the ones God would have us invite. Then we went door-to-door, until seventeen people had promised to attend. We also arranged for babysitting and a child evangelism program for the children since there would be twenty-three children coming too.

The evening was a tremendous encouragement to our faith. We invited Ann Wall, wife of a local dentist, to come and share her testimony. In a quiet, unassuming way, she told how Jesus Christ had revolutionized her home. Four of the group invited Christ into their lives, and the next week Lea started a Bible study in her home. "Now it seems like the whole neighborhood has changed," Lea had told me. "That coffee really broke the ice. All around women are opening their hearts to me. They are anxious to talk about spiritual things. These were the same women who hardly spoke to me when I passed them a few weeks ago."

That June, Virgil graduated from dental school. He and Lea applied to OMS and were accepted as missionaries to Haiti. As candidates, they faced a staggering challenge. They would be required to raise full support, enough funds to cover all personal and ministry needs for five years plus another $6,000 for Virgil's dream of a Haitian dental clinic.

As I pondered the challenge Virgil and Lea faced, I found myself asking, *Lord, what can I do to help?*

How about using the coffees? the answer came back. Why not use coffees to get people involved in reaching a world for Christ? Invite neighbors to come over some evening and meet the missionary, have the candidate share his testimony, and then give people an opportunity to be involved in that ministry by sharing in his support.

It was the first step of a plan that God would use to help put scores of missionaries on the field. *Well, why not, Lord,* I said. *That first coffee was a monumental flop, and yet you brought good out of it. Turning weaknesses and failures into strengths and blessings is what you specialize in.*

I sat down with Lea, and together we listed the names of

thirty-five people we wanted to invite. Then carne the important part – getting a verbal commitment from as many of those thirty-five as possible. I picked up the phone and began calling, feeling at first uncomfortable, like a nagging telephone salesman pushing magazine subscriptions.

Lord, I said, *keep reminding me this is for your glory and for your kingdom.*

"I'm having my sister and brother-in-law over to my house," I would begin. "I'm wondering if you would like to join us and hear how Christ is working in their lives and about their plan to go to Haiti. Also, we can get better acquainted." Some of the contacts had conflicting engagements, but many responded positively.

"Look, Leon, I need your help," I announced to my son the afternoon before that first coffee for missions. "I am expecting maybe thirty people tonight. I want you to set up the chairs."

"Good grief, Mom, thirty!" Leon protested, falling back onto the sofa. "You'll never get thirty in here."

"Maybe not," I said, "but I want thirty chairs ready if we need them. Just stack them up."

That night, twenty-five showed up. We sat them on dining room chairs, the piano bench, and the folding chairs Leon had brought over from the OMS social hall; five eased themselves down on our long, low, comfortable sofa. After coffee, a snack, and an informal get-acquainted time, I asked Virgil to tell something of the direction God had given to Lea and him.

Virgil began by recalling his youthful encounter with Jesus Christ. He talked about his decision to study dentistry and then went on to describe how Haiti had broken his heart, leaving him with a burden to build a dental clinic there.

As he spoke, I scanned the faces around the room. Skepticism had melted into friendly appreciation. Other faces seemed to reflect a deep conviction. God was using a simple testimony of all-out commitment to Jesus Christ to create spiritual hunger.

As Virgil continued, I suddenly heard an ominous cracking sound. It was coming from the leg of our overburdened sofa, which wobbled pitifully for an instant, then collapsed unceremoniously and deposited its five occupants on the floor. *Lord,* I shot up in prayer, *what now? This is not the way I planned it at all!*

But my confusion and embarrassment were swallowed up by the waves of laughter that engulfed our gathering. With the sofa propped up, Lea began sharing her testimony, telling how her own vision coincided with her husband's. Then the questions came from the floor: What can we do to help you get to Haiti? How about building the clinic? Do you need help with that?

That was the beginning of our mission coffees. Families and individual women began opening their homes. "Come on over," they would urge their neighbors. "We're having a friend here that we'd like you to meet. They have shared Christ overseas and would like to tell how he is relevant to their own lives and to people of other cultures."

I hardly dreamed how God would one day use this simple idea of neighborhood coffees to help scores of missionaries get to the field, and in the process, restore homes and reshape many lives, mine among them.

7

A Celebrated Grief

While God continued to bless my own life through the ministry he had prepared for me, I struggled at home with my two growing children. I was encountering the often dizzying effects of trying to be a successful single parent.

The year we moved from Los Angeles to Greenwood, Leon had turned twelve, Lorna ten. The following year was Leon's thirteenth, and as though right on cue, subtle yet alarming changes began to take place. What had happened to the sweet-tempered, quiet little boy, who was usually eager to please Mom in spite of occasional ruckuses with his sister?

Suddenly in Leon's eyes, Mom had become Public Enemy Number One. When his tall, gangly frame, topped by a head of thick black hair, appeared in the doorway each afternoon after school, the atmosphere of our apartment became charged with tension. With hardly a grunt in reply to my artificially cheerful, "How was the day?" he would retreat to his room to blow his trombone in noisy protest.

When I insisted he straighten his room, which increasingly looked like a disaster area, littered with the debris of books, pieces of artwork, a dismantled radio, he shot back glares of resentment. "Why are you always on my back? You never treat Lorna this way."

Gifted musically, Leon was well on his way to mastering the trombone and guitar, but now his musical tastes veered toward harsh contemporary sounds with a frenetic beat. Entering the living room, he would turn off the easy-listening station I preferred, supplanting it with a rock station at almost full volume.

"Mom, does it have to be so loud?" Lorna would shriek.

When I objected, Leon would fix me with a hurt look that seemed to accuse, "Go ahead. Order me around. Treat me like a little kid. Take away the little joy I have. Just make me more miserable."

Every mother feels pain when she realizes she must relinquish her boy in order to let him become a man. Now, when I would throw an arm around Leon in an affectionate hug, he would pull away, obviously feeling uncomfortable. And kisses from Mom were certainly taboo.

He now regarded the kitchen as a female domain, and my efforts to enlist his cooperation in the dishwashing chores began to meet with resistance. Leon was thirteen, acting as if he was twenty-one. More and more, he sought subconsciously to be the man of the house, but didn't know how. When I had women friends over for a meal or invited them to a family outing, Leon smoldered with resentment, as though another adult presence somehow threatened his place of leadership in the family structure.

"Hey, Mom!" he exploded one day after my friends had left. "If you want to have your friends over all the time, I think I might as well move out."

Increasingly Leon began to challenge my authority. *Why should he always be obliged to submit to someone who had so many shortcomings herself?* he reasoned. Overnight he had acquired an amazing acumen, a gift for ruthlessly discerning every inconsistency in adults, and particularly in me. He was not slow to point out these inconsistencies.

"Well, how come you are asking me to take out the garbage this week, when last week you said I didn't have to?" he would ask.

"Oh, I forgot that, Leon," I would respond lamely.

"Yeah, Mom, and that's another thing. You have a terrible memory. You are always forgetting things."

I had heard from other mothers that girls are usually easier to raise than boys. Now I discovered what they had been talking about. While from the outset Lorna had been endowed with an indomitable will, this personality trait had been balanced with level-headedness, a generous portion of good sense, and a sunny disposition that made her a friend to everyone.

Affectionate and warm as Lorna was, there was an obvious, intimate mother-daughter bond between us, which gave rise to Leon's accusation, "You always favor Lorna." Spending time with Lorna provided a panacea for all her problems. So we did things together; we cooked, sewed, raised dogs, and worked on Child Evangelism projects.

While Leon was moody, Lorna was outgoing, action-oriented, full of initiative, and self-confident. From her father, I thought, she had inherited strong leadership qualities, combined with a fertile imagination. Her creative mind teemed with ideas – a cookout, an impromptu drama, a pajama party.

Responsible beyond her years, she had proved herself a trusted babysitter, and on one occasion, she cared for a neighbor's children for a month while the woman completed her master's thesis. At school, she exceeded any parent's expectations and had even skipped a grade when we had moved to California. She habitually respected authority figures, parents, teachers, and yet had the strength of character to disagree with a teacher who used vulgar language in class.

In short, Lorna was a model daughter – the kind of sister

my struggling Leon could not help but resent. The summer following his freshman year, Leon announced, "You know, Mom, I think I'd like to leave home." And then he added wistfully, "I really would leave home if I could support myself." He said finally, "But since I can't yet, I guess I'll just have to stick around."

Repeatedly, as I imagine many a baffled Christian parent has done, I would retreat to my bedroom and fall on my knees, pouring out my heart to God. *Lord, how I need Henry now, and Leon needs him. Where are you in all this, Lord? I am so weak. Right here, Lord, in this business of parenting, I need you to take my weakness and turn it into your strength. I need answers. I don't know what to do. I have never raised adolescents before. What am I doing wrong? Where do I need to change? You said in your Word, 'If any of you lack wisdom, let him ask.' Well, I lack wisdom, Lord. And I am asking.*

Gradually, insights came, and I began to make some changes. I realized I had always seen myself as a "helping person." In my unique roles as mother and leader of the home, I had always tried to be a peacemaker, but had been reluctant to show a firm hand in exerting leadership and giving clear direction. I learned that kids need limits and confident direction.

Now, when it came to matters I felt were essential to their personal growth, instead of asking, "Do you want to do this or that?" I said, "I *expect* you to do this." There wouldn't be many rules, but I would be consistent in enforcing the few I made. These rules would be laid down without apologies: loud music for only one hour, no TV during dinners so we could hold intelligent conversations. Surprisingly, Leon and Lorna accepted my new stance. In fact, they seemed to welcome it.

Keeping the lines of communication open, a basic principle in all human relationships, is not easily achieved when dealing with adolescents who suddenly have a penchant for privacy. Still, I would work on it. "How did school go today?" often inspired monosyllabic responses. But I discovered some topics provoked at least a modicum of intelligent oral response – sports, music, certain school activities, and their friends. I even discovered Leon was actually interested in politics.

Next came the hard part. *Confess your faults to one another,* the Bible says (James 5:16 KJV). But did that mean that I should confess them to my children? I decided it did. They had already detected plenty of human frailties in me and had seen through my phoniness; why not talk about those frailties and solicit their help?

With God's help I did. I admitted my faults, yes, my sins, to my own children. I confessed those sins and asked for Leon's and Lorna's forgiveness. I soon discovered that hearing Mom confess her faults gave them the freedom to acknowledge problem areas in their own lives.

Finally, God showed me I needed to place Leon's future entirely in the Lord's hands. Was I hanging on to a dream that Leon would someday be a minister like Henry or at least a full-time Christian worker? In my circle of friends, having a child in the ministry or on the mission field seemed to be the ultimate parental accomplishment. Could I accept Leon as a salesman, an artist, a secular musician? *Lord, I surrender,* I prayed. *He is yours. Do with him whatever you want. I just ask that he love you, live for you in whatever career you have chosen for him.*

God was teaching me through my frustrations with Leon. He seemed to be saying, *Can you praise me for what I am doing in Leon? Praise – by faith – even when you see little to be encouraged about?* As I cultivated a thankful, praiseful heart, I began to notice positive qualities in Leon, and I learned to give sincere compliments without embarrassing my son or myself.

"Would you like to know what Leon shared in our youth meeting last night?" one of the young people from church asked me one day.

"Of course," I replied.

"Well," he continued, "Leon said, 'I miss my dad a lot, but I am finding that Jesus can be closer than a dad, and he's my best friend.'"

Leon began to use his musical gifts to express his love for Christ. He, Lorna, and a neighbor, Cindy Burr, started singing together. They joined The SPARCS, a church musical group, often in demand for Christian concerts. Their exuberant music in praise to Jesus Christ regularly brought troubled young people to the Savior.

Friends commented on leadership qualities they saw in Leon. He was elected president of the church youth group, and he enthusiastically performed on a winning Bible quiz team. An aptitude test indicated that he had outstanding abilities in verbal skills and music. "Mom," he announced one day after a stirring address by Korea missionary Dr. Ed Kilbourne, "I think the Lord may be calling me to Korea as a youth worker."

"Lord," I whispered, "I see you are still in the miracle business."

Praising God for such miracles came so easily. Yet the miracles also provided a painful contrast to the sudden deaths of Leon and Lorna. Thus, when the uniformed officer appeared at my door that cold February evening, the full impact of his words gradually penetrated my brain with a violent, paralyzing force. "Your children and their friend have just been killed." It was as though I were standing outside myself, a spectator to some gruesome drama. Certainly, in a moment, I would awaken from the nightmare.

With Danny and Henry, the valley had approached more gradually. With them, I had time to prepare, to brace myself for the dark, irrevocable finality of the loss; but this time the valley had come upon me suddenly, sucking me down, down into the blackness in one vicious gulp. And yet, even as my brain reeled under the impact, deep from within my being welled up the sweet, mysterious consciousness of the Presence, the everlasting arms: *Yea, though I walk through the valley of the shadow of death, I will fear no evil* (Psalm 23:4 KJV).

Thus, the words came almost unbidden to my lips, "Officer, I know where they are. They are with God." As I closed the door behind me, a surge of comfort also came from the realization that God had prepared a spiritual family to stand with me in my hour of trial. *Who should I call first? Flo Rickards.* Flo had stayed with Lorna on our world trip. Through the years, she had been a friend who had worked with the church youth and had been close to the children. I picked up the phone. "Flo," I began shakily, "the children have just been killed in an accident. I need you. Can you come?"

Flo came, as did my precious neighbors, Les and Pat Ike; my boss, Merv Heebner; and his wife, Clara. They embraced me, and we wept together and prayed. Only those who are part of the body of Christ can know and understand the sweetness of this kind of consolation in the dark moments of life.

When news reached my sister Lea in Haiti, they were entertaining a team of laymen visiting the field on an evangelistic crusade. Immediately, the crusaders took up an offering to fly Lea home. Ordinarily flights were fully booked and reservations had to be made well in advance, but on this day, it "just happened" that one seat was available. When Lea came in the front door, and we embraced, she could sense that God was already doing something special. "Valetta," she said, "why you, of all people? I don't understand it, but I know God is doing something eternal for his glory, and I can already sense he has done something special in you."

I sensed at this time I was being supernaturally sustained by the Spirit of God and by the supporting, consoling love of my spiritual brothers and sisters. Still, a dark shadow would now and then flit across my mind. *Soon,* I thought, *I will come*

crashing down, crushed and wounded and helpless. I felt I would
be haunted, as though an old wound had been freshly opened; I
would again experience the void left by the loss of my firstborn
and the depression that came in the wake of Henry's death.
Then God spoke a word of gentle rebuke. *If I can sustain you
today,* he said, *can't you trust me with tomorrow?*

As news of my children's deaths was broadcast on TV and
radio and conveyed by phone to friends all over the world, I
sensed that I was being borne aloft on a surging tide of prayer
and love. I have never known love like that. The world seemed
literally to be dripping love, oozing at every pore. Was this the
mysterious essence of Calvary – that love in all its sublime glory
that can, in mortal minds, only be understood when there is a
cross? I wondered if others could discern the divine paradox
the Spirit of God was enacting in the mortal life of Valetta
Steel: that God never loves his children so dearly as when he
lets them suffer. He never walks with them as closely as when
he escorts them through the valley.

As I knew myself the special object of the love and prayers of
God's people, I felt humbled as never before. What had I done
to deserve this? Nothing, absolutely nothing. It was all of him,
and suddenly, I grasped the meaning of grace in a new way.

The morning following the children's deaths, I felt as though
God had pulled back a curtain and let me peek into heaven. It
was all joy. Leon and Lorna were there, saying, "Mother, won't
you share our joy? Dad is here and our brother too. We're celebrating. Won't you celebrate with us?"

As I envisioned the funeral, I began to feel a growing conviction that it should be a glad celebration. Leon and Lorna knew
Jesus and loved him. They had lived for him unashamedly and
had shared his Good News with others. Their Lord had summoned them (who are we to say prematurely?) to their blessed
and eternal home. Was that not cause for celebration?

But I hesitated. Some would not understand. What would they think of a mother who wanted to celebrate her children's deaths? Crazy? Unnatural? Morbid? Irreverent? Could they see what I saw? Later that morning, a group of young people from the church came by. I shared with them the idea of turning the funeral into a celebration. "You know," they responded, "that is exactly what we have been feeling. We hesitated to suggest it, not knowing how you would react."

So we planned a celebration. The SPARCS would sing some of the joyful, exultant songs Leon and Lorna had loved, and I invited our Men for Missions friend, Tom Gold, to sing "The King Is Coming."

Flo Rickards accompanied me to the funeral home. When the caskets were opened, I felt puzzled. What had they done to Leon? Had his face been so mutilated that they needed to rebuild it? Whoever it was in that casket, it did not look like my son. "Is his hair combed right? Does he look natural?" the mortician was asking.

"Something is not right," I muttered. "This is not Leon, is it?"

Flo put in, "There is some mistake." Indeed, there had been a mistake. In the aftermath of the accident, Leon's body had been switched with that of his friend, Don Prock, and sent to Don's home in Iowa.

So now arrangements had to be made hastily to rectify the mistake. This could have been very upsetting had my heart not been soothed by the comforting knowledge that Leon had already discarded his earthly shell and was now enjoying the freedom and perfection of his resurrected body.

Leon and Lorna's celebration was a triumphant, joyful, and unmistakable witness to their faith and was all that we had envisioned it would be. Afterward, several young people from church approached me. "I hope you won't misunderstand what I am saying," one began, "but it is a good thing it was them and not me because they were ready and I wasn't. I was faking it, but I want you to know that today I completely surrendered my life to Jesus Christ." Others told how, as a result of the children's deaths, they had recommitted their lives to Jesus.

Dr. Long, a professor at Greenville College, wrote, "Although we cannot see it with our finite minds, we know God never makes mistakes, and only eternity will reveal the total results of this seeming tragedy. It has affected every student in the school, we believe."

The morning after the funeral my phone rang, and I heard the voice of a troubled young woman on the line. "I saw a newspaper on the floor and was startled," she said. "Could it really be your children?"

"Yes," I replied, "they were my children. It is a terrible loss, but I am celebrating because they are with Jesus and were ready to meet him."

Then I heard sobbing. "You know, Mrs. Steel, I'm not ready to meet Christ," she said. I invited her over to my house, and that afternoon she prayed and asked Christ into her life.

As everyone who has studied the subject of grief knows, the most difficult time comes after the initial impact of the tragedy and funeral subsides, and the bereaved is no longer the object of special solicitous attention. The shock wears off, and life must go on; but how to go on in a world irrevocably changed and made stark and strange by the new uncomfortable, gaping holes created by the absence of beloved personalities?

But God had given me a promise in that hour when I had felt the love of his people pouring down upon me. "If I can take care of you today," he had whispered, "can't you trust me with tomorrow?" Well, now "tomorrow" was here.

The Spirit once more directed me to the book of Job, and again, for the third time in my life, those precious Spirit-ordained passages performed their divine function. *Why are you using your ignorance to deny my providence?* God had said. *Where were you when I laid the foundations of the earth? Tell me, if you know so much* (Job 38:2, 4 TLB). No, there is no way that men can fully understand or fathom the providence of God. That is why he has given us the gift of faith, to believe and to leave those mysteries in his hands until the final unveiling.

I turned to James 5:11: *We know how happy they are now because they stayed true to him then, even though they suffered greatly for it. Job is an example of a man who continued to trust the Lord in sorrow; from his experiences we can see how the Lord's plan finally ended in good, for he is full of tenderness and mercy* (TLB).

What I did for Job, God seemed to be saying, *I am going to do for you.*

The sudden death of a loved one, particularly by accident, leaves surviving relatives with a vague, sometimes remorseless sense of guilt. Had I somehow been remiss in my parenting? Too trusting? Too permissive?

Whatever the circumstances in the accident, I found comfort in the fact that I had raised my son to be a responsible young man. He had proven himself to be a careful driver, demonstrating good judgment and integrity ever since he had received his driver's license as a high school junior.

Other thoughts intruded as I did a mental playback of the children's lives and mine. Had I been a wise Christian parent, helping my kids establish their priorities, helping them sort through the confusing choices of life, distinguishing the petty from the eternal? God comforted me with the thought that the most important things had been done; Leon and Lorna had been pointed to the Savior, and they had shared their faith.

The absolute finality of death has a marvelous power to, in one swift stroke, adjust one's scale of values, which is often lost or confused in the helter-skelter process of modern life. How I thank God now that amid the relentless demands of my life, yes, even the ceaseless demands of Christian service, I had learned the importance of leading my children to a personal faith in Jesus Christ. I remember the day Lorna had asked, "Mommy, how can I know I am a Christian and that I will go to heaven when I die?" I was profoundly grateful now that I had not put her off with a vague answer, but had been willing, able, and eager to lead a little child, my child, into God's kingdom.

I had honestly strived to make Christ the centerpiece of our home, and though I had failed many times, I was grateful now that I knew God honored the weak. He had enabled me to confess my faults to my children and ask their forgiveness.

What inexpressible comfort were those indelible memories of Leon and Lorna, alone in their rooms, pouring over their well-marked Living New Testaments. Though they had both been top students, what gave me joy now was the knowledge that they had counted the business of sharing Jesus with a classmate more important than getting an A in chemistry or English. Now there were no regrets that I had consistently taken time for friendship with my children – for cookouts, raising dogs, sewing, long conversations, even debates about sports, music, politics, and religion.

If there is one message I would like to shout to every parent, it is this: Every day that you live out your life before your children, you are imparting to them an entire value system, and what a phony set of values many patents dump on their children. Even Christian parents model lifestyles characterized by money and material possessions. Such are vain and transient baubles when set in an eternal perspective. The fulfillment of selfish ambition and the brief, fickle applause of man – how futile they will appear someday when seen in the light of eternity.

Death underscores the truth of that time-worn couplet,

"Only one life, 'twill soon be past, Only what's done for Christ will last."

If you think you can convey that truth to your child on the strength of a sermonette or on an easy, pious exhortation, you are mistaken. There is only one way that they will understand it, believe it, accept it, and begin to live it, and that is when they see you consistently modeling a Christian lifestyle. Whatever else life may consist of, living unashamedly for Jesus Christ and making the sharing of his Good News with a lost world the first item on our agendas models sound priorities.

8

REASONS OF THE HEART

As I share my testimony in churches and homes and at women's retreats, the question I am asked most often is, "After all you've been through – losing a child to leukemia, a husband to Hodgkin's disease, the sudden death of your two remaining children in an automobile accident – after all that, how can you retain your faith in a loving God? How can you go on smiling, praising the Lord, talking about his goodness? It doesn't make sense."

I answer that nowhere in Scripture are we told that because we are God's children we will be spared the harsh realities of human life. The Bible says, *Yet man is born unto trouble, as the sparks fly upward* (Job 5:7 KJV). Though God showers blessings and goodness upon us without measure, it is also true that his very Son, the one he loves most, is the one he allowed to suffer the most.

God wants us to share in the character of his Son. So, even though suffering offends our shallow, human view of a loving God, the Christian who has passed through the fire learns with Pascal a high logic: "The heart has its reasons which reason cannot understand." In the business of spiritual heart surgery,

God's keenest instrument is suffering. Why? Because only in dying do we learn to live and only in relinquishing everything do we know what true gain is.

Since God loves us and only allows good, we can only understand suffering in the light of the resurrection. Resurrection power means that something positive will arise from all suffering for the Christian, just as Christ arose from the dead.

Another by-product of pain is the increasingly sweet discovery of the Holy Spirit as a Comforter in the life of God's child. Many Christians are timid and ineffective because they have not grasped this truth.

I like to think of it this way: We all have had times when we have felt low in spirit, despondent, discouraged. Then we have entered a room and found a group of friends who know us, understand us, and love us. As we've sat there in that company, we've felt warmed by their friendship and love, reaching out to us with invisible arms to embrace, soothe, and uplift. That is parallel to the ministry of the Holy Spirit in our lives. If we recognize him and meditate on God's words of wisdom, allowing him to perform his divine work, he will be there always, teaching, encouraging, comforting, uplifting.

Why does he do this? We read in 2 Corinthians 1:4 that he is the one *who comforteth us in all our tribulation, that we may be able to comfort them which are in any trouble.* We also read, *You can be sure that the more we undergo sufferings for Christ, the more he will shower us with his comfort and encouragement* (2 Corinthians 1:5 TLB).

Without the presence of Christ and his Word, I would at one time have viewed suffering as punishment. I would have responded with anger, resentment, bitterness, self-pity, and depression. However, since the Word has taught me that suffering is positive, I have looked for those positive results so I can follow God's directions in 1 Thessalonians 5:16-18: *Always be joyful. Always keep on praying. No matter what happens, always be thankful, for this is God's will for you who belong to Christ Jesus* (TLB).

When others ask me how to handle the long dark tunnel of despair caused by separation and suffering, I try to encourage them to develop three simple attitudes. First, develop a grateful heart by focusing on all God is going to do for you through suffering.

Our character is developing (James 1:2-4). We will know Christ better (Philippians 3:10). We still have better things ahead (Hebrews 10:32-34). Our troubles are small and short compared to our eternal blessings and glory (2 Corinthians 4:17).

Second, do as Robert Schuller so aptly instructs: "Turn your scars into stars." In every problem, there is a new opportunity for creative ways to reach out to others for Christ. However, to find that opportunity, we must let go of the past.

Third, discover eternal priorities and become committed to sharing Christ at home and through world missions. Millions of people are waiting for their first chance to hear of Christ.

After the homegoing of Leon and Lorna, I found I had more time to give to the coffee ministry I had stumbled upon with Virgil and Lea. I wanted to reach out to neighbors, and I was increasingly convinced of the effectiveness of the ministry in involving lay Christians in the enterprise of missions.

God was using these home coffees not only to break apathetic hearts for a lost world, but also to bring unsaved neighbors to himself. I longed to give myself more fully to this work, and I shared the burden with my supervisor, Merv Heebner.

One day, Merv called me into his office. "Valetta," he said, "we feel God is doing something significant through your home meetings and that he would have us release you to give more of your time to the ministry if that is what you feel he is leading you to do. How would you like to write your own job description?"

Soon, OMS established a home-meeting department. In the next five years, more than one thousand families registered to become involved in home coffees for missionaries.

The next ten years took me to hundreds of homes and churches in many states. I marveled as God used the simple home coffee concept to involve thousands of lay Christians in outreach to their neighbors and friends. Families developed friendships that expanded their interests across oceans and cultures.

During these years, deep in my heart an idea had been growing that fills my life with energy and excitement. It took shape in Youngstown, Ohio, when Gary Persing, a student at Ohio State University, asked me, "If you were the only Christian in the world, would the world have a chance to hear?"

The answer to that question focuses on the importance of one individual, any individual. If you and I could disciple one Christian every year to become a missionary, and that Christian would disciple one person a year to become a multiplying disciple-maker among peoples where there is no witness, in thirty-three years, one person could reach more than four billion people with the Gospel. Unfortunately, at the present time, it takes 2,500 Christians in America to produce one missionary. As we follow God's command to disciple others, teaching the Great Commission, not everyone responds, so it seems we all need to disciple many to see more workers out in the dark areas of the world.

Because of this vision for more workers, I believe recruitment of young people for missions is high priority, and I sought opportunities in this area. To know there are young people who have never heard of Christ seems the greatest tragedy in all the world and somehow makes my problems seem very small.

As opportunities came for me to speak on Christian college

campuses on behalf of overseas careers, I wanted to increase our follow-up of those who were interested.

Then, in 1983, an opportunity came for me to experience a short-term mission in English evangelism in Taiwan, primarily to make my recruitment ministry more credible. However, in Taiwan, my heart filled with love for the Chinese people, and the Lord showed me a ready opportunity for discipling among new converts at the OMS center in Taichung. Here was the opportunity to prepare workers among a portion of the largest segment of the world's population, the Chinese.

9

A CHINESE CONNECTION – TAIWAN

I was unprepared for the response I received in Taiwan. In my first English Bible conversation class, students brought gifts, invited me to their homes, to festivals, to mountain hikes and feasts, waiting patiently for opportunities to practice simple conversations. They asked, "What is the Bible about? Who is Jesus Christ? How do you find peace? What is the meaning of life? Why is there suffering? How do you know there is a God? Why wasn't Jesus Chinese? Can I come to your home Bible studies?"

The spaces in my heart, formerly filled by my own children, God was filling. I did not want to leave.

The two months stretched into years. The home coffee ministry changed to a home Bible study ministry for myself and in guiding many short-term workers in beginning bilingual Bible studies. I had the joy of joining the OMS Chung-Tai English Ministries, which included participating in a daily English broadcast founded by Ed Erny on 17 major stations, English camps, follow-up rallies, and a Night Institute directed by Sylvia Knapp.

Judy Lee, a general's daughter, opened her home for Bible studies. She tied up the dog, answered the phone, poured the tea, interpreted, took care of her family, and reached out to scores of women. Many in her Bible study have traveled to China to share Christ, as well as reaching their families and neighbors.

Bonnie Tsai, Leah Chen, Grace Shiah, Lucy Chen, and scores of other Chinese women worked as my interpreter and co-workers. Today they are bright lights, working among Chinese people.

I had read the apostle Paul's words: *But life is worth nothing unless I use it for doing the work assigned me by the Lord Jesus—the work of telling others the Good News about God's mighty kindness and love* (Acts 20:24 TLB). On hot days, driving my motor scooter to a home Bible study, my heart was filled with the joy of a deep life purpose and sense of meaning. These words and activities, I thought, have eternal consequences impossible to imagine.

One weekend after much prayer, Bonnie Tsai's parents, both of whom had worshiped idols their entire lives, came to Christ. A few months later, Bonnie's mother said, "I need to buy a washing machine because I need more time for church visitation and Bible study."

Pauline Chen, who had been driven from her home because she accepted Christ, wrote one Christmas, "I have received my best Christmas gift. My parents now accept me and we are reunited."

Connie Lee once showed me two photo albums full of people who had come to Christ during her missionary journeys to closed countries.

People ask, "Why is it so important to teach the Bible and involve people in ministry?" Discipling is more than a class – it is life involvement. How we need each other's concern and prayers in the valleys!

The next valley demonstrates the great need missionaries have for prayer. Was my life to be an object lesson, showing God's power through answering prayer and helping me forgive?

10

ANOTHER VALLEY, ANOTHER VICTORY

Breaking the Crystal Ball

In March of 1990, I returned to Taiwan after six weeks of
ministry in the United States. I was eager to join in the training of more than 100 young collegians coming to Taiwan in
June. These Western youth would be teamed with Asian youth
to take the Gospel to seven nations around Asia. That night, as
I headed across the seminary campus to my house, I could not
have imagined the dark and awful tragedy about to engulf me.

Gorgeous blossoms of pink bougainvillea covered the long,
open front porch of my home. Entering the kitchen, I noticed a
shadow dart across the wall. Peering into the laundry, I saw a
human figure, slightly stooped. Was this person ill? Was he or
she a Bible school student or a friend of one of my housemates?
Three short-termers, April Armstrong, Karen Kwong, and Carol
Wagner, lived with me in the old three-bedroom house. Only
a few minutes earlier, it seemed, they had grabbed their lesson
plans and hurried off to their English Bible classes.

"Why are you here? Are you okay?" I called out.

Suddenly a man in a jogging suit lunged toward me, grabbed my wrist, and, at the same time, turned out the lights. Desperately trying to collect my wits, I cried out in Chinese, "Jesus loves you, and I am praying for you."

Despite my struggles, the man pulled me into the bedroom. When I screamed, he flung me to the floor and shoved a pillow over my face.

With a surge of terror, I realized both his intentions and my utter helplessness. All I could do was remind the Lord that my body belonged to him. The intruder then raped me and left me alone in the still-darkened room.

Trembling, I hurried to my missionary neighbors, the Bettingers, who called our Chinese coworker, Daniel Chang. The police were notified. As dozens of uniformed officers descended on our campus, Daniel characteristically seized the opportunity to share a Christian witness and a tract with each one. God gave me special strength as I described the incident and went to the hospital for an examination. Though I thought it unlikely that my attacker would be apprehended, I agreed to press charges if the culprit were found.

In the days that followed, Satan assailed my mind. Was the Lord powerless? Could it be that he had some purpose in allowing this nightmare? As I pondered the Scriptures, the Lord took away my confusion and filled my heart with peace. I was grateful the younger women were unharmed. Covered by his blood, I was assured that I was still pure before him and that this loathsome, crucible experience would be used to prepare me for his work in some new way.

The next Sunday morning in my devotional study, 2 Corinthians 1:8-11 seemed just for me:

> *I think you ought to know ... about the hard time*
> *we went through in Asia. We were really crushed*
> *and overwhelmed, and feared we would never live*
> *through it. We felt we were doomed to die and saw*
> *how powerless we were to help ourselves; but that*
> *was good, for then we put everything into the hands*
> *of God, who alone could save us ... and he ... saved*
> *us from a terrible death; yes, and we expect him to*
> *do it again and again. But you must help us too, by*
> *praying for us. For much thanks and praise will go*
> *to God from you who see his wonderful answers to*
> *your prayers for our safety! (TLB).*

I began thanking the Lord for saving my life. Later, I learned that my assailant was a violent man who had even committed murder.

As I prayed, the Lord encouraged me to share the experience openly and seek prayer, not only for myself but also for our planned evangelistic outreach and the protection of all our workers.

That morning, after I prayed for ways to be a witness, a group from the police station came to bring flowers and fruit. Grateful that my first testimony book was available in Chinese, I gave copies to the police chief.

As I shared my ordeal with my entire Taiwan missionary family, God came into our midst, releasing tears and prayers and binding us closer than ever. Telling the Chinese staff, however, was harder. Not wanting them to lose face, I assured them that this violent act could have happened just as easily in America as in Taiwan. They, too, wept as God melted us together, giving new unity and purpose.

Our ladies' Bible class interpreter, Judy Lee, came to pray with me. Should I tell her? Would she think God had failed me? Or would she accept it by faith? How my heart rejoiced when she said, "Romans 12:1 states that we are to present our bodies as a living sacrifice. Many young women in your Bible classes have experienced abuse and their hearts are bound by unforgiveness and anger. Possibly the Lord wants to deepen your ministry to these young women."

I thought, too, of a possible ministry to the most abused of women – the prostitutes in Taiwan who number several hundred thousand.

The response of my sister, Lea Ullom, a missionary nurse in Haiti, brought precious consolation:

> As I pray and weep before the Lord that He placed such a cross on you, I cannot help but agree that somehow He, for a time, lifted His wings enough to allow Satan's attack, to open for you even deeper ministries. Jesus said He would not take us out of the world, but would keep us in the world. That means we can be subject to accidents, illnesses, and other attacks of evil. But, we're promised that Satan will not be allowed to do more than God permits, as in the case of Job.

> My prayer for you and for me is that the devil receive no glory, and that fear will not linger in your heart and mind.

> In the Old Testament Hannah said, *I have been praying here out of my great anguish and grief* (1 Samuel 1:16 NIV). In answer to her cry, God gave the miracle birth of Samuel. Perhaps it takes anguish and grief to "birth" the miracles so desperately needed in our world today.

Already, God has revealed portions of his purpose in allowing my traumatic experience:

> The accused rapist, thief, and murderer was appre-hended – a man created in God's image but now bound by Satan's illusions. From a dysfunctional family, divorced father of a young son, he said a "spirit" came over him whenever he saw pornogra-phy. Divine grace enabled me to join Daniel to visit the man on death row. "If you died today, would you go to heaven?" Daniel asked him.
>
> "No, I will go to hell," he answered.
>
> "If you wanted to go to heaven, what would you do?" Daniel continued. When he replied that he didn't know, Daniel shared the Good News and gave him a Bible and our Bible correspondence course.

Beyond protecting me from death and disease, God granted the miracle of a forgiving heart. I praise him for Calvary and his example of forgiving those who crucified him. He also pro-vided loving friends and counselors who listened. The shame no longer remains, because my body is his possession. Now he continues to provide opportunities for giving hope to the brokenhearted, so they, too, will prayerfully seek to be used of God to heal others.

Our mission team, though deeply shaken by the incident, continued all their summer ministries with zeal. Living "on our knees" and taking God's full "armor" (Ephesians 6:11-16), we sought tools for spiritual warfare. As our team met together, we focused on some of the following:

> A pure heart: *If we confess our sins, He is faithful and just to forgive us our sins and to cleanse us from all unrighteousness* (1 John 1:9 NKJV).

The anointing of the Holy Spirit: *If you then, being evil* [as compared to God] *know how to give good gifts to your children, how much more will your heavenly Father give the Holy Spirit to those who ask Him* (Luke 11:13 NKJV).

God's wisdom: *If any of you lacks wisdom, let him ask of God, who gives to all liberally and without reproach, and it will be given to him* (James 1:5 NKJV).

God's protection and help of his angels: *Are they not all ministering spirits sent forth to minister for those who will inherit salvation?* (Hebrews 1:14 NKJV).

A grateful heart: *Rejoice always, pray without ceasing, in everything give thanks; for this is the will of God in Christ Jesus for you* (1 Thessalonians 5:16-18 NKJV). Gratitude and generosity stood against the greed and abuse that seem so prevalent worldwide.

A generous heart: *But as you abound in everything—in faith, in speech, in knowledge, in all diligence, and in your love for us—see that you abound in this grace* [the grace of giving] *also* (2 Corinthians 8:7 NKJV).

Realizing that because of our strong commitment to evangelism and church planting, we were under severe attack by Satan, we affirmed our victory according to Revelation 12:11: *They defeated him* [Satan] *by the blood of the Lamb and by their testimony; for they did not love their lives but laid them down for him* [Christ] (TLB).

My niece, Tami Ullom Myer, learning of the ordeal, wrote the following:

WET SCARS

Pounding the floor
  of the throne room of God,
kicking my feet,
  screaming my heart,
I demanded to know
  how this could be:
No, God! No! No!
  Lying still then, exhausted,
in my anger, I wept.
  In the Great Hall of God,
I heard only silence
  Til finally hushed, I heard
the drop of tears.
  Looking up from the floor,
I saw the nail-pierced feet;
  I saw them
drenched in tears.
  I was in the presence of the Heart
that knew greater pain,
  greater compassion,
greater sorrow,
  greater mercy,
than my puny heart could ever know.
  And in stillness, I lay
worshiping,
  adoring,
at those scarred and wet feet.[1]

Will my mind be plagued by fear or will it be consumed by the love of God? Every day as I awake, my favorite verses tell me of his love. In this meditation, I become certain of five attitudes.

1   Used with permission.

And because God has no favorites, they are also for you. Centered on Jesus' death on the cross, they bring deep inner healing.

> I am DEEPLY LOVED. *For God so loved the world that He gave his only begotten Son that whoever believes in Him should not perish but have everlasting life* (John 3:16 NKJV).

> I am COMPLETELY FORGIVEN: *If we confess our sins He is faithful and just to forgive us our sins* (1 John 1:9a NKJV).

> I am FULLY PLEASING. Jesus said, *"As the Father loved Me, I also have loved you"* (John 15:9a NKJV).

> I am TOTALLY ACCEPTED. *For by grace you have been saved through faith* [in Christ] (Ephesians 2:8a NKJV).

> I am COMPLETE IN CHRIST. *For in Him dwells all the fullness of the Godhead bodily; and you are complete in Him* (Colossians 2:9-10a NKJV).

My Chinese coworker, JoAnn Chang, dreamed she saw my heart in a crystal sphere. The sphere was broken, but my heart still beat with the love of Jesus. Yes, that is God's miracle.

That summer proved to be our most productive ever. More than 1,000 people heard the Gospel, many for the first time. Some 100 made solid commitments to Christ. Through the Asian student outreach, 140 young people from many nations were trained to evangelize and gave their summer in seven Asian countries. As a result, thousands of lives were impacted for eternity. As I corresponded with several of these young evangelists who hoped to return some day, I saw a great need for prayer and support systems that would offer encouragement through training and developing a base of support.

Compelled of God, I returned to the States on a mission to help equip and prepare new candidates.

In September 1991, after many painful goodbyes, I left my home in Taichung. Driving past the familiar markets, high-rise buildings, mountains, and rice paddies, too quickly we arrived at the Taipei airport. A new chapter in my life was beginning.

En route home, I stopped in South Korea. Known for its vibrant churches, this land held special memories of former visits. I was met at the airport by dearly loved missionaries. J.B. and Bette Crouse talked about Korea and J.B.'s new assignment as OMS President, and then they excitedly told me of their recent trip to Russia.

Arriving in Greenwood with a new position designed to train, provide coaches, mentor, and serve new missionaries, I found myself praying, *Lord, what part do you want me to play in reaching young people with your love?*

A short time later, J.B. Crouse announced that OMS was joining The CoMission – an association of 80 evangelical organizations responding to the Ministry of Education's invitation for missionaries to assist Russian teachers in teaching Christian Ethics and Morals. Their goal: to train 12,000 teachers by 1997.

In June 1992, at a workshop for new workers, I met Bill and Nancy Kidwell. Bill had learned the Russian language in the military and served in Germany as a Russian language translator. "We've been praying for years that the door to Russia would open to the Gospel," they said. "Now we are eager to go."

Nancy Kidwell and I presented a women's prayer seminar in Wilmore, Kentucky, entitled, "God's Answer for Broken Hearts and God's Answer for a Broken World." One of our special guests that day was Russian educator Klara Krasill, who encouraged us to translate my book, *Thrice Through the Valley*, into Russian. She offered to assist us in the first printing. Once the book was published, letters like the following began to come:

Dear Klara,

I'm afraid my long-time practice in that bureaucratic commercial style has eaten up all normal everyday human words. That book you gave me last week ... I didn't refuse it because I tried to be polite. I hardly ever read anything related to religious subjects because this kind of literature seems to me too moralistic, or too boring, or else too dogmatic.

So at home I opened that book just of idle curiosity ... to get an idea of your translation style. I soon forgot all that. The book carried me along and turned to be so gripping that I "swallowed" – I mean devoured – the whole of it at one go.

I find it too hard to explain in English, but even in Russian it would not be much easier I think. It (*Thrice Through the Valley*) has made an atheist read the Bible in a completely different way – not just as a literary relic but as something much more profound and mean-ingful. The story is so astonishingly frank and open-hearted, and touching, and horrible, and encouraging at the same time.

I just cannot imagine how she could stand all that, how she survived ... I gave the book to Tanya. She read some to her mother, and so it went further on ... You start thinking your misfortunes are nothing ... This (book) is very important, especially for those who are unfortu-nate, unhappy, and who cannot see any purpose in life.

Out of four generations in our family, my little Anna is the first to be taught the Bible. (How can we) ... describe how unintelligible, obscure, and awkward that teaching often is – just because there are not many ... who can teach such delicate things. —Olga

*****

Dear Ms. Valetta Steel,

Your book shocked me. It's written with emotional language people understand. Your life, the grief which you had to survive, and how you overcame the trials can be an example, a consolation for many people in Russia.

There are answers to many painful questions: Why do I have to suffer so much? Why can't I be happy? I think your understanding of God's Word and its incarnation in your life helps many people believe in God and not to grumble at the suffering, which He sends us.

I want to give this book to others for consolation and advice. Unfortunately many Russians lost their very connection with God. We were educated as atheists and pursued and persecuted His servants. Now the Russian people are looking for God. Thank you very much for this book. —Maria, a student of the college

*****

This book saves people from suicide and loneliness. When I read this book, I can't help but cry. But these are not ordinary tears. These are tears of happiness that Christ will never forsake me. Valetta, dear sister, many are asking for your book. It gives us God's answer to suffering. —Elena

*****

In August 1993, God allowed me to participate in the training of 250 Christian educators preparing to leave for various cities in the former Soviet Union. Countless prayers for Russia were being answered.

11

WALKING IN THE MALL IS
GOOD FOR THE HEART

Snow crunched under my feet as I ran out to start my old Oldsmobile. The dim morning light hugged the horizon. Soon I was walking briskly past the shops inside the warm Greenwood Mall – my morning exercise before a long day at the office. After nine years overseas, I felt like a stranger in the United States, so when OMS coworkers Juanita Bertolet, Ruth Hunter, and Arlene Ashton invited me to join them in their morning mall walks, I thought, "Why not? Maybe I can get readjusted to the States and renew some old friendships."

Reading Psalm 68:5-6 that morning brought comfort: *He is a father to the fatherless; he gives justice to the widows, for he is holy. He gives families to the lonely* (TLB).

"Lord," I prayed, "Thank you for my many friends and the missionary family I work with, but you know about the lonely spaces in my life. May my heart be so focused on you, I won't notice those lonely spaces."

While I strode toward the mall exit, a gentleman stopped me. "Do you remember me?" he asked. Surprised, I struggled to place this somehow familiar face. Al Crumley. Yes, I remembered.

In 1972, after the children's accident, Al had come to a seminar I led. Later, on several occasions, we met for lunch and talked about grief. Since he was a widower, I sensed he may have been interested in getting better acquainted. I remembered what he had said. "When you return from your next trip, give me a call."

But when I got back to Greenwood, I was hesitant. With my present commitment to world evangelism, I wondered if I should allow anything to distract me. Later, I heard Al had remarried.

"Al, how is your family?" I asked.

"My wife passed away last year," he said. "I am in that same situation as when we last talked – going through grief. Do you suppose we could get together?"

An awesome sense of God's presence came over me, similar to those moments after my children's accident. It was like God's enormous peace, and almost audibly it seemed God was saying, *Maybe you can't figure this all out, but I am in this – don't be afraid to open your heart.*

Dinners out, walks in the park, meeting family and friends, worshiping and praying together, our friendship grew. Al and I discovered how much we had in common. We both had grown up in conservative Free Methodist homes, lived in California, the Northwest, the Midwest, and Asia. We both enjoyed travel, photography, sports, family gatherings, and being with friends. Al had always wanted to be more involved in missions. As we dated and shared our feelings, our love grew. On June 2, 1994, we were engaged.

On September 24, 1994, following his fourth short-term mission to World Gospel Mission's hospital in Kenya, Africa, we were married in Al's lovely home. A reception at the Community Church of Greenwood followed. That day, God blessed me with a loving husband, four children, their spouses, and five grandchildren. In Christ, we are all becoming great friends.

A medical doctor, administrator, and pharmaceutical

specialist with Eli Lilly, Al Crumley is now retired. His home is three miles from the OMS office where I work, and his long-time avid involvement as a photographer is put to good use in OMS as we travel in ministry.

How good God is to bless me with a loving husband who is also a personal doctor, administrator, counselor, chauffeur, and most of all a prayer partner. Yes, I believe our marriage was made in heaven.

How beautifully God fulfills his promises and satisfies our deepest longings. His loving ways are veiled in mystery as we walk in this world.

For as the heavens are higher than the earth, so are my ways higher than your ways, and my thoughts than your thoughts (Isaiah 55:9 KJV).

12

THE BEST IS COMING!

We see woven through the entire Bible the crimson thread of God's promises and the depth of their meaning. Though some promises are for a specific time or place, another set of promises is for all time. Though our faith will be tested, God is always faithful to keep his promises.

The Bible tells how the human race deteriorated morally after man's rebellion. When God told Abraham to leave his kinfolk and journey to a new land (Genesis 12:1-3), he gave him four major promises that were repeated to his descendants. These promises, which include blessings to all nations, are the center of Bible history. How can these promises give us new confidence?

One of the promises made to each of us is the gift of righteousness or a "great name." Names in Asian culture have great significance. *God will credit righteousness – for us who believe in him who raised Jesus our Lord from the dead* (Romans 4:24 NIV). No one can take away this gift, even when our character or name is attacked. This gift of righteousness is promised by Jesus in Matthew 5:6: *Blessed are those who hunger and thirst for righteousness, for they will be filled* (NIV). No valley can take away our gift of a righteous name through faith in Jesus.

God also promises to make everyone who believes in him a great blessing. That implies he will need to work on our character and through our weakness. Now I can see how God has taught me to depend on him through the valleys and the mountaintops of life. He is giving us, as partners, impact in blessing all nations. These promises fulfill our inner longings to make a difference. You, too, are chosen in Jesus to bless all nations as you live faithfully and compassionately.

We also read that righteous Job was tested. What was the outcome of his testing? Job 42:10, 13, 15-16 tell us that his end was better than his beginning.

Does God fulfill his promises? My personal testimony is a huge YES.

I believe we must remember, at any age, **the best is yet to come. He promises us a place in his new, eternal kingdom where all suffering will be over.** Some day soon, we will all stand before Jesus Christ. Will he be our first love? Will the investment of our time and talents reflect his love for us and our response?

Will you allow his love to flow through you? You, too, can experience the hope found in Ephesians 3:20-21: *Now to Him who is able to do exceeding abundantly above all that we ask or think, according to the power* [Jesus' love] *that works in us, to Him be glory in the church* [his body] *by Christ Jesus to all generations, forever and ever. Amen* (NKJV).

If you'd like an explanation of how to know God in a personal way, please make sure you read the Afterword in this book. As his love flows through you, it will then be your turn to write his story through your life.

Epilogue

You've read part of the journey, but it continues. I'm humbled by his grace and answered prayers.

When heavenly angels carried Danny, then Henry, then Leon and Lorna to heaven, I cried out, "Lord, you've left me. How can you put my life together? What is your plan?" I felt like a ship without a rudder or a car without a steering wheel. I kept looking up and the Lord gave me hope, watching his plan in my life unfold as a part of his larger purposes.

Remember God's open door to Russia, our involvement in training, the Russian printing of our book, people going to teach morals and ethics in the Russian schools? The five-year CoMission commitment would quickly end, and then what would happen? Thousands prayed. Sasha Tseutserov, a member of the KGB, spied on his daughter learning English from a foreigner. He heard the teacher reading Matthew 7:11 *And if you hardhearted, sinful men know how to give good gifts to your children, won't your Father in heaven even more certainly give good gifts to those who ask him for them?* (TLB). Sasha thought, "I'm a hardhearted, sinful man and I love to give good gifts to my daughter." He began reading the Bible only to find Christ and dedicate his life to the ministry.

The CoMission had arrived in Russia, and Sasha joined in a

church fellowship with OMS missionaries. He shared the heartbreaking fact that Communism had closed more than 100,000 churches and killed thousands of pastors. OMS, under J.B. Crouse's leadership, in partnership with Dr. Alexei M. Bytchkov, founded the Moscow Evangelical Christian Seminary. For 20 years, Dr. Bytchkov was known as a major influence in the life of Russian evangelical Christians. Sasha, eager to prepare for ministry, attended Asbury Seminary in Wilmore, Kentucky, and then moved to Scotland, where he earned his Ph.D. Now the former KGB officer heads Moscow Evangelical Christian Seminary and is involved in training pastors and planting churches. Regularly Sasha returns to the States to assist in raising scholarships for the Russian ministerial students. What a joy for me when he shared his testimony in our local church.

Won't your Father in heaven even more certainly give good gifts to those who ask him for them? (Matthew 7:11 TLB). Those very same words often burned into my heart. Did God want to give me more ministries if I would only ask him? In answer to prayer, God opened another door for a ministry in Russia. Kara Krasill, a Jewess from Russia, was an atheist – until she met Bill and Nancy Kidwell in Kentucky, part of the OMS team assigned to Russia. They, in turn, introduced her to the Bible, which led to her belief in Jesus Christ. Later, at a retreat, she received my first book, *Thrice Through the Valley*. Deeply impressed, Kara sensed the potential and need in Russia for the story of triumph through tragedy. Determined to make it happen, she returned to her country and not only translated the book but also published and aided its distribution. She translated for me some of the letters she received.

During the days of the CoMission, Bruce Wilkinson's book, *The Prayer of Jabez,* became a best seller. Jabez teaches us to pray for ourselves unselfishly in 1 Chronicles 4:9-10.

I copied an adaptation of it for you and me from the

Discipleship Journal. Placing it in my Bible, I breathe it often. I found the Lord answering in powerful ways.

PRAYER OF JABEZ

Dear heavenly Father, Please bless me indeed.

Enlarge the scope of my ministry for you and culti-vate my life in prayer.

Expand my faith in your word and amplify my vision for your Kingdom.

Gracious Master, Bestow your power, Manifest your presence and

Grant Your protection every day. In Jesus' name, I pray.

—Garth Leno

BRITISH ISLES SURPRISE

Billy Campbell, OMS representative in the United Kingdom, wrote, asking if I would come to the British Isles for five weeks. Shortly after that, Al proposed. What should I do? I was excited about opportunities of ministry, meeting the special people of that area, and the travel. I approached Al, not sure of his response, saying, "Would you like to take a ministry trip with me to England, Ireland, and Scotland?" I knew Al loved photography, so I added, "Would you like to pack your camera and do a photo trip?"

We had not announced our engagement, so I called Billy Campbell. I knew housing arrangements would need to be adjusted. I said, "Billy, could I bring a prayer partner with me?"

He said, "Of course, what is her name and would she like to be involved?"

I said, "It is not a woman. It is a man and he will be my

husband." I had been a widow for 31 years, and Billy Campbell, who never lacked for words, was speechless. Al took hundreds of great pictures and shared how God led us together. We saw the Lord touch lives, and hundreds were reading *Thrice Through the Valley*.

NEWLYWEDS TRAVEL TO AFRICA

Al was eager for me to visit Kenya, where he had served as a volunteer doctor at World Gospel Mission's Tenwek Hospital on five occasions. I watched with pride as Al saw a stream of patients daily. Franklin Graham of Samaritan's Purse arranged our logistics. They literally assist hundreds of medical personnel to find the best short-term service opportunities in mission hospitals so dependent upon their help. At the close of our stay, the hospital arranged a safari for the volunteer doctors. Al, who had been an avid photographer since his childhood, could hardly wait until we jumped in a jeep and headed off across the jungles looking for lions, giraffe, elephants, wildebeests, rhinos and more. The camera went click, click, click.

DR. AL GOES ON A SHORT TERM MINISTRY IN TAIWAN

After our trip to Africa, Al was eager to go with me to Taiwan, where I had spent nine years. He met my missionary family, Chinese coworkers, and friends who had been in my classes. He became a counselor to some older men in his first English camp. A highlight for him was traveling across the lush, green, steep, rocky mountains, and through the Taroko Gorge. We could look down thousands of feet from narrow winding roads, hoping rock slides would not deter our travel. We caught our breath in arriving at the beautiful East Coast in Hualien, the mountainous area where the aboriginal tribal people settled. This area was once considered the land of the headhunters. I praised the Lord for the way he used OMS and friends I had known working in that area. At one time I took a group of Chinese women to Prayer Mountain, a place where the Chinese of many churches go to worship, fast, and pray. I commented that the praise groups sounded so heavenly and different from the usual Chinese music. My Chinese friends said the mountain people are known for their clear voices and beautiful music.

OMS work in Taiwan began as Japanese missionaries were sent by the OMS-related Japanese churches. Through these missionaries, Komod Kabala An, the son of a powerful head-hunter chief, came to Christ. Because of the tribal practices, he was unwilling to seek a wife from among them. The Japanese missionary sent word to the leaders of the OMS-related seminary in Tokyo, asking if there would be a seminary student who would go and marry this redeemed son of a headhunter and assist in reaching the tribal people. After a time of prayer and fasting, one of the most promising young women in the seminary surprised many and answered God's call to go. She took the amazing journey to Taiwan and became the redeemed headhunter's bride. Together they spent their lives ministering among the aboriginal tribes with the amazing blessings of the Lord. Al and I visited a museum village, which was dedicated to the tribal people and showed their former customs with rows of skulls as a reminder of the past. That practice no longer exists.

CANTON, OHIO, CONNECTS TO KOREA

Chung-Soon Sue Kang sent me a surprising letter. I had traveled to Canton, Ohio, for a meeting in the home of Sue Kang, wife of surgeon Dr. Wook Kang. As I drove, I prayed the Lord would manifest his wonderful presence. I had never met the Korean woman, but I knew she was a friend of an OMS missionary. I finally found the beautiful home. It was breathtaking, with charming oriental hanging lights and Asian décor. The room filled with women. I shared my story of Christ's faithfulness through the valleys; then I ended with prayer. There were tears as well as smiles at the close. After some days, I received the following letter.

Dear Valetta,

Praise the name of our Lord who gives us the final victory in any circumstance.

I also praise the Lord for your life where is the evidence of His existence, the fact that He is in control. It is such a comfort knowing that the same God who upheld you through so many valleys would carry me in my journey too.

I don't know whether you remember me. You had come here for a home meeting. I felt that I saw the genuine joy and peace about you even before I learned of your story. I later wondered in my heart whether that was really possible as people in the Bible rejoiced in the time of tribulation.

As I read along in the book, I almost felt compelled to translate it into Korean so that Korean people would have a chance to hear of the Lord's working in a person's tragedy. There are so many immigrants living in America, struggling in the midst of "money is everything" society. They also have the loneliness of being different, not being able to freely communicate. I have a burden for the Korean women … I have translated one book, DAYBREAK into Korean.

I put this matter onto the Lord … I just feel a strong desire to have my people read this book.

Love, Chung-Soon Sue Kang

The Lord guided us to ask Sue Kang to translate the book. In South Korea, Dr. John Hong, the OMS liaison person, and Sarah Kappler, an OMS missionary, worked together to accomplish the printing. It was an amazing joy for Al and me to travel to Korea to share my testimony in Korean churches and at Seoul Theological University, one of the largest OMS-related Christian training centers in Asia. After the chapel, I had the joy of signing several hundred books for the Korean students. It seemed so miraculous that we would be there.

Dr. Al, a former U.S. Navy doctor during the Korean conflict, recalled many memories of earlier days in Korea as a Navy doctor. Everywhere we went to minister together, the Koreans thanked him for his military service. They were grateful that the United States had helped save their country.

I also remembered being in Korea in 1963, seeing the Korea Evangelical Holiness Church in action. We hopped into OMS missionary Elmer Kilbourne's jeep as he sped over bumpy roads, first to one orphanage and then another, talking rapid fire about how they came into being. Elmer Kilbourne and his close friend Bob Pierce wept together over more than 100,000 destitute orphans. They developed a partnership that grew beyond imagination. Bob Pierce said he would help raise the funds for the orphans and destitute, if Elmer could direct a program where Korean Christians would manage the day-by-day care. Bob Pierce later went on to form World Vision.

Kilbourne came to the States yearly, and I would hear him spew out facts like a machine gun, trying to squeeze reports of what God was doing in Korea into his allotted time. He ably directed the huge orphanage and feeding programs, and in addition, he conceived an amazing land reclamation project to provide land to orphaned young men when they graduated. He was awarded some of the highest honors that a nation can bestow upon a foreigner; however, he was always eager to give the Lord the credit.

Elmer's life deeply challenged my faith. Back in Greenwood when I became a part of the OMS Book Ministries Committee, we were excited to see Elmer's story published – *Missionary Maverick* by Ed Erny with a forward by Franklin Graham. Franklin said, "Elmer Kilbourne has been a great friend to me over the years ... Seeing Elmer's passion and enthusiasm for mission work has always motivated me to consider the possibilities of what God can do through lives that are 'sold out' to Him."

Al and I were filled with emotion as we looked over the city of Seoul and saw hundreds of red crosses in the sky, signifying churches. As Christians investing in missions, we see that investment multiplied in South Korea, their own churches now sending out thousands of missionaries.

JAPAN

One night as I sat upstairs in my home office, the phone rang. A woman was weeping. Though she had a slight Asian accent, she was calling from Kentucky. She said, "An OMS missionary gave me your book, and I began to read it but couldn't put it down. It is touching my heart, speaking to so many things I've gone through. I think this book will help many Japanese people, and I want to translate it for them."

I learned that she was the gifted "voice" or interpreter for a Toyota CEO. That began a friendship, and the book was translated into Japanese. After it was printed, the OMS-related church in Japan, the Japan Holiness Church, invited Al and me to come for three weeks of meetings throughout Japan. Chiharu flew to Japan to travel as our interpreter. Doors to churches and homes opened for us to share God's amazing grace.

In one of the first meetings, a young Japanese man, who was diagnosed with cancer, came and asked for prayer. God opened the door to the hearts of the people, and we could not help but love their kind and gentle ways. We were invited to return again for ministries two years later.

We heard the plea for more missionaries. Dan Iverson, Japan country director with Mission to the World, says there is only one church for every 16,000 people. Japan continues to be one of the least reached countries in the world.

COFFEE, CANDLES, AND CARING

OMS missionary to Republic of Ireland, Marian Byrnes, had a ministry dream. She and husband Larry, wanted to plan special events across Ireland for people who had been grieving for years and did not know how to get out of their grief. They asked if I would come and do a series of women's events in hotels, small towns, and churches. OMS missionaries Luci Long, with a rich alto voice, and Karen Hogrefe, who had served with the CoMission and at OMS headquarters, would complete the team. The Irish planning team began to see answers to prayer, and the schedule filled. Doors opened in hotels, churches, restaurants, and homes.

We served coffee, Luci sang, and I shared my testimony and principles from God's Word to comfort the grieving. We invited the people to have coffee, dessert, and talk or pray – whatever they wished. All our team was busy at various tables, sharing and praying with the women that attended. The last event was a Sunday evening church service, and we again concluded with coffee, dessert, fellowship, talking, and praying. The sharing and praying lasted until nearly midnight.

In a culture steeped in religious tradition, we discovered many did not understand a relationship with Christ. Many feared that their deceased children might be in hell. They did not know the Scriptures in which Jesus said *Let the little children come to me, and don't prevent them. For of such is the Kingdom of Heaven* (Matthew 19:14 TLB). Also, in Matthew 18:10, Jesus said *Beware that you don't look down upon a single one of these little children. For I tell you that in heaven their angels have constant access to my Father* (TLB).

Is the Republic of Ireland a mission field? We learned it has the lowest percentage of evangelicals of any English-speaking nation. OMS is currently seeking missionaries to serve there.

HAITI EARTHQUAKE

On January 12, 2010, buildings collapsed, and cement walls and roofs crashed, burying people in the rubble of the worst earthquake ever to hit Haiti. Thousands lost their lives, and thousands more were left homeless. People wanted to help. Bible school students started tent churches in the tent cities. OMS began sending teams to build homes. The Lord's nudging kept a thought coming to my mind. Would my book be helpful to people who had lost families? Could it be translated into Haitian Creole? Haiti missionaries suggested I ask Storly Michel, the Haitian director of the OMS radio station, Radio 4VEH, if he would consider translating the book. He agreed, and after many months of work, the book was translated and then printed in Haiti. When I heard that the book would soon be coming off the press, I began praising the Lord for using the valleys in my life to comfort others.

In June 2013, Storly invited me to Haiti. Radio 4VEH would celebrate its 63rd anniversary, and Storly suggested it would be a great time to introduce the new Creole book. Walking to the platform of one of the largest churches in Haiti, packed with thousands of Haitians, I felt humbled among so many who had lost family members and loved ones. I trusted the Lord to use a simple testimony of my hope in Christ. I wanted to proclaim the love of Jesus on the cross and how he faced the pain, suffering, gloom, and despair for us. The Bible teaches that the power of the Holy Spirit that brought Christ from the tomb is available to us to help us through the valleys and forward on the upward journey. Afterward, Haitians came to tell me of family members they had lost. We prayed and wept together.

The next day, we climbed into a truck with a team to travel to a remote village where we would share the plan of salvation and the gift of solar-operated radios, pre-tuned to Radio 4VEH. Bible school pastors assisted us. Our team contacted thirty-eight people, gave out twenty-five radios, and presented the Gospel twenty-seven times. Eleven people prayed to accept Jesus. Wow! That ministry continues and is a great opportunity. Is a new day coming in Haiti?

For two hundred years, the dark cloud of Voodoo has hung over Haiti. When the slaves revolted and gained their independence, they dedicated Haiti to Satan. As the 200th celebration of that dedication approached in 2004, government celebrations seemed to be in disarray. Prior to the event, Christians in Haiti and the United States passionately encouraged prayer and unity. A great rally was planned in the sports arena in Port-au-Prince with the intent of "breaking the curse of Voodoo and dedicating Haiti to Jesus Christ." Many ministry leaders from the States came to participate, and the sports arena filled with people. One speaker, Dr. J.L. Williams, preached Saturday night, quoting Luke 10:18: *I was watching Satan fall from heaven like lightning* (NASB). He also preached on 1 Corinthians 10:20-21 *I do not want you to be participants with demons. You cannot drink the cup of the Lord and the cup of demons too; you cannot have a part in both the Lord's table and the table of demons* (NIV). They had two tables on the stage, one representing the cup of demons and one the cup of the Lord. They smashed the one representing the cup of demons, followed by communion and symbolically dedicating Haiti to Christ.

What was it like for me as I returned after 30 years? I believe the prayers and unity of God's people are breaking the curse of Satan. I was overwhelmed with the maturity and giftedness of the Haitian leadership. Will their godly influence assist in meeting the great spiritual and physical needs in the poorest nation in the Western Hemisphere? The dental clinic started by my brother-in-law, Dr. Virgil Ullom, is now led by nine Haitian workers; the medical clinic is now staffed by 65 Haitian workers; Emmaus Biblical Seminary now has 50 students preparing for ministry. Radio 4VEH, with Haitian leadership, received the National Religious Broadcasters award for outstanding programming and ability to relate the Gospel to the culture.

Haiti's future today is different because hundreds of missionaries obeyed God's call, lived in conditions to which they were unaccustomed, and discipled Haitian leaders. In addition to training pastors, radio workers, and medical personnel and distributing solar radios that include the New Testament in MP3 format, OMS has a child sponsorship program, Starfish Kids, which assists hundreds of Haitian children in receiving a Christian education and thus preparing those who will one day be the leaders in Haiti.

THE PHILIPPINES

In Evansville, Indiana, I met Pastor Bill Oden and his wife, Joyce. They had read *Mission Accomplished Under Sentence of Death,* the story of Henry Steel. After reading this book, Pastor Bill invited me and the OMS team to host a mission's event in their church. Later, I was invited to assist Joyce Oden in an outreach coffee where we saw the Lord work in the lives of a number of women.

A few months later, I heard with joy that the Odens had felt called by the Lord to join OMS as full-time missionaries. A short time before I flew to Taiwan, they sensed God's call to help begin the work for OMS in the Philippines. When I traveled from Taiwan to the Philippines to renew my visa, Bill and Joyce welcomed me to their home. They were beginning Bible studies. We prayed together as they shared their challenges. There were no OMS-related churches and no Bible training center.

Other missions in Manila were reaching the poor and begged OMS to target an unreached group, the upper class. Joyce realized that Filipino women, just like other women all over the world, had an interest in beauty, so she trained in color analysis. Joyce found a ready response among the affluent. As she taught classes followed by color consulting, opportunities came to build relationships and begin Bible studies. A year after Joyce began using Master Design, a biblically based program that used color analysis as a starting point, a group of missionaries and Filipinos hosted a luncheon with a beautiful fashion show and more than 160 women attending. Afterward many expressed interest in joining a Bible study or a Master Design class. The church began to grow.

More than 20 years later, Al and I traveled to the Philippines for ministry. We saw a packed church with more than two thousand Filipinos worshiping Jesus. The church was led by a pastor trained in the OMS-related Faith Bible College. We shared in the Bible school retreat and in a retreat for the church staff. The enthusiasm of the people being trained to plant churches and serve as missionaries thrilled our hearts. Years earlier, in the meeting at Joyce's home in Indiana, it was beyond imagination the amazing ways the Lord would guide their lives as well as ours. In 2014, Joyce completed her biography, *Snapshots in Time,* a beautiful book filled with stories of God at work in the lives of TV personalities, business people, and the humble poor from under the bridge.

TRAVELING THE TRAIN IN INDIA

In 1963, when Henry and I traveled to India prior to his death, fewer than 25 OMS-planted churches existed. Recently, Dr. Wesley Duewel handed me a copy of some notes he took of a sermon Henry gave in 1963 when he preached to a group of 700 missionaries in Landour, India, just weeks before he passed away. Duewel said:

Six years ago, a brilliantly successful young pastor was told he had Hodgkin's disease and perhaps 2-5 years to live. He asked his denomination to assign him to a job related to missions. They said he was too valuable as a pastor. He came to OMS. He said, "I know I am a dying man. Valetta and I have talked it over. Before you say anything, here is our signed statement that we want no medical aid. All we ask is the privilege to give ourselves fully to missions until I die. It may be years or it may be months. Use us in any job you want; I only want to do something for missions before I die, for I am convinced missions is the biggest thing in God's program today."

Weak, coughing, and tired when we arrived in India in 1963, Henry was not the only one suffering. Hundreds of hungry people crowded the fences around the airport, slept in the hotel hallways, begged for food, and lived in hovels alongside those more affluent in the upper caste. My heart was broken with all the suffering I saw and felt. I was forever changed.

When Dr. Duewel returned from India for a home ministry assignment, he pleaded with people to pray. I remember wanting to respond to that appeal. His goal was to enlist one thousand people to pray for India at noon every day. He told of traveling all day on bicycle from village to village without meeting a single person who had heard of Christ. *Operation World* states that in India, of 159 people groups with more than one million people, 133 are unreached. Hundreds more groups of fewer than one million people are unreached.

In a difficult environment of idol worship and hostility, God is raising up spirit-filled leaders – teachers, pastors, church planters, social workers. The Evangelical Church of India (ECI) today has more than 10,000 churches (5,500 of which are house churches) and 13 Bible schools. They send over 700 Indian missionaries to the unreached ethnic groups of India. Their goal is to plant 100,000 churches with one million believers. When I realized that these pastors often face persecution, I felt humbled and honored when Ezra Sargunum, the bishop of ECI, asked me to briefly tell of God's grace in the valleys at their largest ordination of 160 pastors.

In 2001, Dr. Al and I traveled more than 60 hours by train on four overnight journeys in India with Dave Graffenberger and Dean Davis. We still saw beggars, people in hovels, and evidence of great need. However, we also saw the hope in the smiling faces of congregations praising the Lord and in young men and women in a number of Bible training centers. India still needs our earnest prayer for the Lord to call workers for the millions who are lost and for the scholarships to train workers, pastors, and church planters.

COLOMBIA

Jeannine Brabon, whom many know as the "Angel of Bellavista Prison" in Medellin, Colombia, wanted thousands of copies of my first book, *Thrice Through the Valley,* to give to the families of prisoners. Her sister-in-law Patricia Brabon, who is Colombian, and Bible scholar Rachel Coleman translated the book into Spanish. With a strong culture of death in the prison and assassins filling the cells, the OMS-related Biblical Seminary of Colombia began a ministry in the Bellavista under Jeannine's guidance. Hundreds of prisoners have come to Jesus and then trained to minister. I was eager for the families of prisoners to understand that Jesus could also walk with them through their valleys.

Eneida wrote from Colombia. "I send a picture to say that

5,000 women of Colombia, God allowed healing in their heart because it has been a blessing to hear your story. It is really only God who does new things in our lives and shows us his love and his compassion. Some women in armed conflict lost their children, their husbands, their sons and even their grandchildren. Thanks to God your book has embraced and showed us his love."

Hmmm. When we're walking through the valleys, how could we possibly imagine God's bigger plan?

ECUADOR

When Al and I arrived in Ecuador, we had the joy of ministering to a former unreached people group, the Saraguro Indians. Today, they are no longer unreached. We sat on a hillside for a women's retreat. They shared their challenges, and we prayed together. As missionaries themselves now, the Saraguros walk mountain paths, taking Jesus to other isolated tribes. They manage a radio station that beams information, weather, and the Good News to many scattered mountain people.

Forty years prior to that trip with Al, my first husband traveled to Colombia and Ecuador as his introduction to OMS. He was deeply impacted by the cruel killing in 1956 of five outstanding missionaries by the Waorani Tribe of the Auca Indians in the jungles of Ecuador. Their stories were told in the news nationwide and through Elisabeth Elliot's books, *Through Gates of Splendor* and *Shadow of the Almighty*. At that time, OMS was considering targeting one of the unreached people groups of Ecuador for mission work.

OMS took a survey among the Saraguro Indians. Hostile to outsiders, no evangelical group had worked with them before, and there was no doctor anywhere in the surrounding area.

The Lord reached into a humble home in Ohio for a pioneer. After high school graduation, Bill Douce started working on his dad's farm. While getting horses from the pasture, he sat on a stump to pray. He heard the Lord saying to him in an almost audible voice, *I want you to be a medical missionary.* Douce did not know any doctor and was not planning to go to college, but he was certain that this was God's call for him. He told his dad, who said he would help him. Following graduation from Asbury College, marriage to Ilene, and medical school, they faced even more challenges: raising support, learning Spanish, and getting an Ecuadorian medical license. While they were raising their support, they heard of the five missionaries killed in the jungle of Ecuador.

After language study, Bill was required to take all the medical exams in all the major subjects in Spanish to get his license. Assigned now to the hostile Saraguros, they rented a part of a building that would serve as a clinic and housing for the Douces, a nurse, and a dental technician. The Saraguros, wary of outsiders, would have their first doctor.

Fermented by a local religious leader and energized by alcohol, 120 Indians wielding clubs and machetes filled the street outside the clinic and began to beat down the door. Their objective was to run the Americans out of town. Brave towns-people came to the defense of the missionaries, and finally the Ecuadorian army from the provincial capital stepped in. With patience and loving service, the Word of God began to find its way into many hearts and lives. The Douces and team members gave their lifetime to build friendships and share the message of Christ. Their ministry was backed by a host of praying and giving partners primarily from Indiana, Ohio, and Michigan.

WHY SHERWOOD, MICHIGAN?

In the tiny town of Sherwood, Michigan, a high school girl came home weeping, "I'm pregnant."

The baby arrived, and she didn't know what to do. Frank

was passed to his Aunt Dot for a couple of weeks and then to his grandparents. After a time, his grandmother Kittie had a relationship with another man, Jack, so they moved to Richmond, Indiana, where Kittie and Jack spent much of their time drinking and gambling. Jack belonged to a club that had a stage and a bar, and the musicians at the club planned programs for the children. They discovered the people loved hearing little Frank sing. Most nights, Frank was featured at the club, and after some time, he was invited to sing on the radio. Frank went to school during the day and spent his evenings at the bar until it closed, sometime between midnight and 2 a.m.

He spent summers with his Aunt Dot in Sherwood, and when he was eleven, Frank did not want to return to Richmond. None of his relatives had room for him, so he decided to try to find a family.

Frank walked down a side street with mostly wood frame houses and lined with large oak trees. Some homes were quite unkempt. He knocked on a door and said, "I heard that you folks might be interested in helping a young boy who would like to stay in Sherwood but doesn't have a home. (Frank admits to making up this line.)

Mr. Williamson answered, "And who is this boy?"

"Well," he said, "It just happens to be me."

And then it happened.

Mr. Williamson said, "Well come on in, and let's talk about it." He then called to his wife, "Helen, There's a boy here who needs some hot chocolate." And Mr. and Mrs. Williamson became his foster parents.

When the Lord called us to Sherwood, I wondered, "Would it not be better to go on to school? Get the college degree?" But the Lord clearly led, and we went to Sherwood, using up our college savings. Frank crossed our path when he was 16. At that time, he reveled in giving Christian kids a hard time. Henry reached out to the lonely, troubled boy, remembering his own childhood. He tried to be the big brother and friend he always wanted. Eventually Frank committed his life to Christ.

I remember the day his foster parents stopped at the house and said to us, "Frank spends so much time here he might as well live with you folks." After we moved to Kalamazoo, that is what happened.

After cancer took Henry's life, I rejoiced in hearing that Frank and his wife, Lyonie, were applying for missionary service. Their first assignment was to Brazil. Frank's next assignment was to serve as the recruitment director for OMS. The Lord expanded his outreach through InterVarsity Christian Fellowship and in Japan and China, recruiting for ELIC (an organization that sends English teachers to Asia). As I spoke with Frank in early 2015, he was preparing to take a team to Brazil that summer.

In 2014, Frank celebrated his 50th reunion at Seattle Pacific University. SPC awarded him and Lyonie the prestigious Medallion Award for their work in taking more than 4,000 young people to the mission field. Frank's gifted singing voice has moved many audiences to consider God's call as he sang such songs as "All He Wants Is You." Sometimes, when we don't understand God's call in our own lives, we can trust that he is working on a bigger picture.

BRAZIL

The Lord opened another door I had never anticipated. My coworker in Greenwood, Gwen Pinkerton, was transferred to Brazil. She promoted the printing of my testimony book in Portuguese and invited Al and me to come and help promote the book. We arrived at the height of soccer season, yet our schedule was full as we shared in Christian bookstores, at a retreat, in churches, and with seminary classes. What a surprise when Frank Gorsline crossed our path as he was there preparing to bring another team. Again, I could see the amazing complexity of God at work in many lives to bring the Gospel to the nations.

BETWEEN VALLEYS AND VICTORIES

Trinity Evangelical Divinity School came to Taiwan. In two concentrated weeks, a person could take several courses. Was the Lord providing another lifetime ministry dream? Since I loved to teach the Bible and was coordinating English/Chinese Bible studies in Taichung, how grateful I was for this opportunity to deepen my Bible training. When I returned to the United States to work at OMS World Headquarters in Indiana, Community Church of Greenwood offered Trinity courses. After plodding along for several years, I had the joy of graduating with Al by my side. Dr. Robert Coleman, who wrote *The Master Plan of Discipleship,* was my counselor. Again it was evident the Lord was keeping his word and planning my life and answering the prayers of many.

I'm grateful for continued opportunities to be involved with discipleship and training new missionaries. We are eager for others to join the teams, praying for the Lord to call workers into the harvest.

THE MIRACLE OF THE FAITH PROMISE

People asked us, "How can you join a faith mission and still pay your bills? What if the money doesn't come in?" That was my question too. We decided to take a daring step of trust, not in our small faith, but in God's faithfulness. We would trust the Lord to bring in the needed support as we ministered and challenged people to embrace the Great Commission. After my first husband passed away, I was reminded that the Lord had provided for all of our needs plus our medical bills. People had taken shares in my support.

Now, the Lord has challenged me to take new steps of faith

in taking faith promises to other missionaries. Some wonder how that is possible on a fixed income, but if "planned on" money can disappear, so can unplanned money arrive. I was thinking about a missionary the Lord had laid on my heart. That day, while driving what I thought was the speed limit on Fry Road, an officer pulled me over and gave me a ticket. My heart fell, knowing I would have to appear at the courthouse. I lifted a prayer. *Lord, you are in control of my finances.* Special courage prompted me to ask, "Where is the "not-guilty line?" I was told to go and speak to the judge. I said "Since there was no sign, I was driving the speed for country roads." He said, "Fry Road is a city road, however, we will forgive your ticket." The next week, I saw a speed limit sign posted on the road. The Lord also told me that was the beginning of my next faith promise.

What is a faith promise? First, it is believing God wants to send missionaries. Romans 10:14-15b says, *But how shall they ask him to save them unless they believe in him? And how can they believe in him if they have never heard about him? And how can they hear about him unless someone tells them? And how will anyone go and tell them **unless someone sends** him?* (TLB, author's emphasis).

Second, I believe he wants to channel resources through each of us as we trust the future to him. Many churches and missionaries challenge people to make a faith commitment of what they believe God would have them give to a missionary or missionaries. In John 14:14, as Jesus prepares his followers to carry on his mission, he says, *Yes, ask anything, using my name, and I will do it* (TLB). Many times, we hesitate for fear we may not have the resources. This is where faith is so dynamic. When we feel the Spirit nudge us to take a step of faith, we can rejoice! Why? We know God will provide. We can join our prayers with our missionary friend, trusting that God's undying love for the lost will work powerfully, providing the resources for them and for us. As God blessed me through participating in faith promises, I was eager to encourage others to participate. I cannot describe the joy it brings. Below is an amazing faith story from someone who still partners in my ministry, as well as others, through her faith promises.

Marcia Thompson understood her Messiah and became a Jewish believer. Since that time, she has eagerly shared her faith around her kitchen table as well as through Bible studies. At an OMS retreat in Flint, Michigan, the Lord worked in Marcia's heart as I challenged women to host home meetings. Marcia responded, and through her home, she and her family were linked to OMS worldwide. She wrote her testimony, entitled "Oil Jar Faith." Here is a portion of it:

> Do I believe this stuff? Often, reading the Bible, I've stopped and contemplated that question. I accept it as truth, but can I apply it to today's situations? Paul, my husband, and I have five children … the Lord has enabled us to endure many trials – several relocations, miscellaneous surgeries, and all that comes with being imperfect people in an imperfect world.
>
> One summer, however, brought a real faith-bender. We had again moved – this time from Michigan to California for an upper management position with an aerospace company. The company laid the "red carpet" for us … with assistance, relocation expenses, and an investment in purchasing our home.
>
> A year later, however, unrest developed in the workplace. Lack of communication and support from the leadership spread like a deadly disease as one by one employees received termination slips. At first, I thought this could not happen to us. After all, we were God's

children who tithed and served faithfully. God would protect his own, wouldn't he?

He did, but in ways far from what I asked or expected. Two weeks before Christmas, Paul and I faced a new experience of unemployment and total loss of social prestige.

Suddenly God's faithfulness to the widow of Zarepheth took on new meaning. Would he fill our "oil jars" too (Kings 17:8-16)?

As I prayed, God gave me a "vision" of two outstretched hands. If we continued to keep one hand open to share with others, he would fill the other, regardless of circumstances. With this assurance, we determined to be faithful in sending monthly gifts to our missionaries and tithing to our church.

Amazingly, in those 18 long months without a paycheck we never lacked food, medical needs, or clothing. Although my husband sent hundreds of résumés and made many phone calls, he had few responses. I cried out to God as David did in the Psalms. Often, tears of anger and grief flowed. But he always gave comfort and grace to go on. Our entire family marveled at the supernatural peace God bestowed.

Groceries showed up on our doorstep and money arrived, often anonymously. Checks came in the mail from friends across the country who sensed by the Holy Spirit that we needed help ...

Watching God fill our "oil jar" became a daily experience ... Paul, now working as a business consultant, travels all over the world.

So, to those suffering financial loss, my advice is to trust. When no answers are in sight, God merely wants sole dependence on Him – not in self or in the world ... Without question, the "stuff" in God's Word can be believed – and applied TODAY in every situation.

... for cheerful givers are the ones God prizes. God is able to make it up to you by giving you everything you need and more so that there will not only be enough for your own needs but plenty left over to give joyfully to others (2 Corinthians 9:7b-8 TLB).

MY MOTHER

My precious mother went to be with the Lord at the age of 105. Over the years, our friendship grew. A friend gave me a great suggestion. For my mother's 103rd birthday, I made a list of 30 reasons that I loved my mother. She was blind by then, so my sister Lea Ullom, living near her in Florida read them to her. I was grateful for this idea, as it meant so much to my mother.

My brother-in-law, Dr. Virgil Ullom, was challenged by Dr. Gary Chapman's book, *The 5 Love Languages.* In a phone call, he said to Mother, "Tell Valetta you love her." She said, "Valetta is my first daughter, and I have always loved her." Hearing those words for the first time after all these years brought tears of joy to my heart. I realized my mother's love language was service, and words were not that important. She was a great mother and was always there for us, cooking three meals a day and meeting our basic needs. That was her way of saying, without words, "I love you."

HOW CAN I THANK YOU

It is impossible for us to thank all of the people that God has used to bless our lives. I'll forever be indebted to many OMS missionaries from whom I've learned much about Christ and his Great Commission. Al and I have visited 22 countries and ministered in most of them. None of this would be possible apart from the Lord's provision and the prayers, support, and encouragement of many godly friends, both here and overseas.

Valetta Stevenson, age 3

Valetta, age 13

Henry Steel and Valetta Stevenson met at Spring Arbor
High School and Junior College in Michigan.

Henry's graduation from Spring Arbor

Henry and Valetta were married in
Temperance, Michigan, on July 7, 1951.

Henry spearheaded a fund-raising campaign to
remodel the Free Methodist church in Sherwood,
Michigan, where he served in his first pastorate.

Danny Steel, age 2, 1952 – 1955

Breaking ground for the expansion site of the Free Methodist church in Kalamazoo

Henry at Mars Hill in Greece

Leon and Lorna Steel

Henry with Korean pastors

Henry Steel, age 32, 1930 – 1963

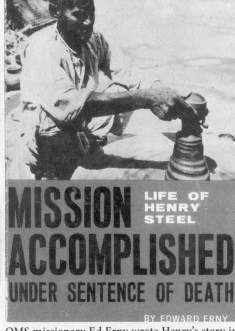

LIFE OF HENRY STEEL

MISSION ACCOMPLISHED UNDER SENTENCE OF DEATH

BY EDWARD ERNY

OMS missionary Ed Erny wrote Henry's story in Mission Accomplished Under Sentence of Death, a book that God used to call people to missions.

Valetta, Leon, and Lorna in Los Angeles

Valetta, Leon, and Lorna, 1965

Valetta's first missions conference after Henry's death, sharing her missionary heart and raising support; front row (l-r): Elma Phillippe, Valetta, Dorothy Backer; back row (l-r): Garnett Phillippe, Bill Gillam, Frank Gorsline, Joe Rogers

Lorna at the piano

Leon was chosen as king at an OMS youth camp.

Valetta's family moved to Greenwood, Indiana, when OMS
World Headquarters moved there from Los Angeles in 1965.

Leon and Lorna joined the SPARCS (Singing Praises About a Redeeming Christ) at West Morris St. Free Methodist Church in Indianapolis.

Leon Steel, age 17, 1954 – 1972

Lorna Steel, age, 15, 1956 – 1972

Valetta's first ministry trip to Haiti

Lea Ullom, Valetta's sister, served with OMS as a missionary in
Haiti at the dental clinic alongside her husband Dr. Virgil Ullom.
The clinic was built in memory of Leon and Lorna.

Valetta traveled to hundreds of homes in Michigan, Ohio, and Indiana to conduct home meetings with missionaries.

Valetta worked with young people in the OMS English Night Institute in Taiwan, which was led by Ed Erny and Daniel Chang. (l-r): Ed and Rachel Erny, Carol and Daniel Chang.

In Taiwan, Valetta also let Bible studies for women and youth in churches and homes.

Valetta, Sylvia Knapp, and Daniel Chang on Taiwan's weekly Good News English Broadcast

Leah Chen (l) and Bonnie Tsai (r), two of the top interpreters in the English ministries, with Valetta

Valetta's transportation of choice in Taiwan

Russian educator Klara Krasill was so deeply moved by *Thrice Through the Valley* that she offered to translate it into Russian.

OMS joined the CoMission and began sending workers to Russia in 1992.

OMS friends hosted a bridal shower for Valetta prior to her marriage to Dr. Al Crumley. (l-r): Eleanor Burr, Arlene Ashton, Barbara Kilmer, Martha Davis, Kathy Heinrich, Ruth Hunter, Juanita Bertolet, Rachel Orr.

Valetta's extended family at the wedding

Dr. Al Crumley and Valetta Steel, married September 24, 1994

Al and Valetta with Al's children, their spouses, and the grandchildren

AFTERWORD

Have you ever been without hope? Maybe you, too, have suffered loss without hope for a better future. As you look at the wars, sickness, and crime around you, have you ever asked, "Does God love me or my country?"

OUR PROBLEM

Though we are created in God's righteous, moral image and though the Bible teaches us that he loves us and desires to give us a life of peace, love, meaning, and purpose, how can we find this life?

The Bible says our ancestors were blessed:

God created man in His own image; in the image of God He created him; male and female He created them. Then God blessed them (Genesis 1:27-28a NKJV).

The Bible says our ancestors lost God's blessing through disrespect. Adam and Eve, our first ancestors, were tempted by Satan to disbelieve God's words to them. They listened to Satan instead and chose the knowledge of good and evil, which includes the understanding and experience of suffering and death. *But God did say, "You must not eat fruit from the tree that is in the middle of the garden, and you must not touch it, or you will die." "You will not certainly die," the serpent said to* *the woman. "For God knows that when you eat from it your eyes will be opened, and you will be like God, knowing good and evil"* (Genesis 3:3-5 NIV).

The Bible says every person has sinned. We have made wrong, independent choices. *For there is no difference; for all have sinned and fall short of the glory of God* (Romans 3:22b-23 NKJV).

For example, just as Adam and Eve sinned when they chose actions forbidden by a loving God, we also sin when we live independently from a loving God, directing our own lives. Every choice has a consequence. *For the wages of sin is death, but the gift of God is eternal life in Christ Jesus our Lord* (Romans 6:23 NKJV).

The Bible says Christ came as a peace offering to bring God's blessings back to those people who listened and obeyed him. This Holy God, in his Holy Trinity (Father, Son, and Holy Spirit), provided his own holy and acceptable sacrifice for our sins. This he did by his own plan, through his only Son, Jesus Christ, the same Son of the Holy Trinity.

By the death and resurrection of Jesus Christ, we are now allowed to approach this Holy God, because we have forgiveness of our sins. In knowing him, we have his peace, his guidance, his strength, and eternal life.

The Bible tells us how to know God personally. God wants us to experience his holy love in an individual way. Therefore, you can receive Christ into your life by faith through prayer. When you do this, God will send his Holy Spirit, Christ's Spirit, from heaven to live within you. You thus receive new life, eternal life from God.

Possibly this prayer expresses the desire of your heart:

> "Thank you, God, for sending Jesus. Thank You, Jesus, for loving me enough to die on the cross for me. I open the door of my life and receive You as Savior and Lord. Thank You for forgiving my sin, coming into my life, and accepting me as your child forever. Be the lover, leader, and Lord of my life. Help me to be like you."

If you have prayed this prayer, please sign your name here and tell someone you are a Christian.

Also, seek fellowship with Christians who believe and live out the teachings of the Bible.

NEW BIRTH – THE PATHWAY TO GOD'S PEACE

When we pray to receive Christ, God gives us new life. This new life is called the "new birth." In the Bible, Jesus answered, *Very truly I tell you, no one can enter the kingdom of God unless he is born of water and the Spirit … You should not be surprised at my saying, "You must be born again." The wind blows wherever it pleases. You hear its sound, but you cannot tell where it comes from or where it is going. So it is with everyone born of the Spirit* (John 3:5, 7-8 NIV).

This "new birth" is not only a proof or witness to God's love and presence but also provides a "new nature" in us, so we can better live for God in a new moral ethic by God's standards. In a sense, we become like a newborn baby on a spiritual level. Once we become "born of the Spirit," we must begin to learn a new way of thinking and living day by day, as we pray and meditate on the person of Christ in the Holy Bible. We then build a personal relationship with the Holy God through Jesus.

In the Bible, Jesus said, *Peace I leave with you, My peace I give unto you: not as the world giveth, give I unto you. Let not your heart be troubled, neither let it be afraid* (John 14:27 KJV).

—Valetta Steel Crumley

Dr. Al, serving on a short-term mission trip at Tenwek Hospital in Kenya

Dr. Al at Tenwek Hospital

Al's first English camp in Taiwan

Valetta with Sue Kang at her husband's hospital in South Korea

Valetta, signing her book at Seoul Theological University after she shared in chapel

Dr. John Hong, professor, interpreted for Valetta

Valetta and Bonnie Tsai with Dr. Wesley Duewel. Bonnie translated Dr. Duewel's book Touch the World Through Prayer into Chinese.

Chiharu Derber, Japanese translator and interpreter, with Valetta in Japan

Valetta, Al, and Japanese interpreter Hatoko Inoue at one of the OMS-related Japanese churches

Valetta shared her story with Irish women in the Republic of Ireland.

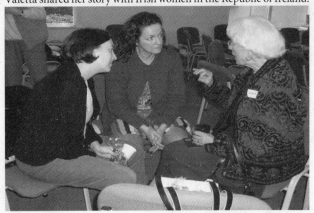

Bill and Kathleen Burnett, then-Northern Ireland regional directors for OMS, with Valetta

Church service in Cap Haitien, Haiti, celebrating the 63rd anniversary of OMS ministry Radio 4VEH, during which Valetta introduced the newly translated Creole edition of her book

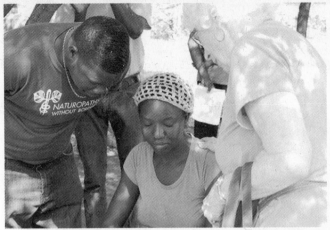

In Haiti, Valetta participated with a team to share the Gospel and distribute solar-powered radios that are pre-tuned to Radio 4VEH.

Al and Valetta, with OMS missionaries Brent and Kim Burdick and students at Faith Bible College in Manila, Philippines

Valetta shared about prayer at the Faith Bible College retreat.

Valetta with Dr. Ezra Sargunum, bishop of the
Evangelical Church of India, and his wife Mangalam

Al and Valetta, with OMS missionaries David Graffenberger
and Dean Davis at a training seminar in Secunderabad, India

While in India, Al and Valetta traveled 60 hours by train,
on four overnight journeys, visiting three training centers.

Saraguro Indians in Ecuador, formerly an unreached people group

Saraguro-owned radio station, reaching isolated Indian tribes

OMS missionaries Frank and Lyonie Gorsline

Valetta with OMS missionary Gwen Pinkerton in Londrina, Brazil; Gwen arranged the printing of Valetta's book in Portuguese.

Al shared marriage insights at a couples' camp retreat while in Brazil.

The OMS-related church in Maringa, Brazil, where Valetta shared her message.

After Valetta shared her testimony in Maringa, she and Al saw a woman reading the Portuguese edition of her book while sitting along the street nearby.

Valetta's graduation from Trinity Evangelical Divinity School with a master's degree in missions.

Valetta's mother, Irene Stevenson

A CHALLENGE TO CHRISTIANS

THE VISION

Aquestion came to me one day that changed my life. It was: "If you were the only Christian in the world, would the world have a chance to hear of Jesus?" The only way we can answer "yes" is to be involved in some way in discipling a disciple maker, no matter what our secular or Christian occupation might be.

Andrew Murray was used by God in the great student missionary movement in the early 1900s. He said, *"IF there were only one Christian in the world, and he worked and prayed a year to win one friend to Christ, and IF these two then continued each year to win one more, and IF every person thus led into the kingdom another to Christ every year, in thirty-one years every person in the world would be won for Christ."* As I considered this truth, I began to refocus my energies. Let me explain.

A Plan with Two Sides

What is this plan? Can you envision a plan with **two sides**, one upward to God and one outward to the world? OMS, as it seeks to plant churches, uses this concept. It is very productive to immediately begin training a new convert to be a disciple maker. Ralph Winter, in his famous Perspectives course, which gives the scope of world missions, describes the upward side as being blessed, and the outward-to-the-world side as accepting the responsibility to bless others.

Can you see these **two sides** as we trace God's plan of redemption through the life of Abraham, the Jewish nation, and then Christ's coming? Christian anthropologists point to Christ, the perfect incarnational model, who was 100 percent God, and who reached out to man 100 percent, as the perfect example of a cross-cultural witness.[1] Jesus was blessed with all of God's nature and then so identified with humanity that through his humanity, he prepared a bridge for man to God. Today that is our pattern in building the body of Jesus worldwide.

Have you observed that biblical knowledge and piety alone, as essential as these are, do not produce the full model of Christlikeness? Have you observed people like the Pharisees who are full of religious knowledge, and yet are rigid, prideful, and legalistic? Was Jesus different? How radical was his life? We swallow hard as we watch him push past the cultural norm, identifying with the brokenhearted people of society. How could we understand his message unless he had modeled it for us, including giving his life to meet our needs?

What was his plan to spread Christianity? He selected the most **F**aithful, **A**vailable, and **T**eachable **(FAT)** men to be with him, to learn from him, and then to pass on his words, his love, and his kingdom plan in transferable ways. How can we follow in his steps? Can we identify **FAT** people and invest our lives in their maturity (2 Timothy 2:2)? As the Lord opened my eyes to pouring more energy into eager learners, this concept helped me see more fruit in my ministry.

Understanding the Challenge

How do people learn? Is it not when the learner actually can put into practice what he/she has learned? God's plan was so effective that it has reached us, yet there is a big job still awaiting us. Consider how Jesus spent his time. He gave most of his time to his disciples, taking them with him in his ministry. He built a deep and loving relationship with each one. Notice that he imported his words and his plan through personal relationships. His disciples watched and participated as he preached, healed, cast out demons, traveled dusty roads, and faced both welcoming and hostile crowds.

Often we find Christians with very low motivation. I recall the time I thought Christian work was mainly for the preacher and the missionary and that I was inadequate for either. When we are encouraged to see our own potential through Christ's empowerment, dreams begin to form. We realize God's commands mean God's empowerment. When we know we can really make a difference locally and globally through his grace, our witness and potential can explode.[2]

Making it Personal

Why is Christ calling everyone? Since more than two billion people have not heard the gospel, Christ desires that every person sitting in the pew allows him to walk in their shoes, speak through their mouth, and minister with their hands. There are enough Christians to reach the world in our generation!

When we walk beside a spirit-filled trainer, we learn. That is what happened to me. I heard many sermons on winning lost people, but felt I did not have the gifts or abilities to win the lost. It was after first listening, learning, and praying, and then going to the neighborhood park with a dynamic woman that I began to see how to implement a personal ministry. Later, I learned that Dr. D. James Kennedy, who began Evangelism Explosion, an organization that specializes in assisting people in leading others to Christ, had been preaching about soul winning with no results. Then he took one person with him in visitation and it happened: The person he took was eager to begin to win souls. The learner – who saw his potential with Christ – was changed. Kennedy saw that preaching and teaching alone was not sufficient to train workers, so he set up a ministry where teaching on the job made the difference. Since then, people all over the world have been trained to share their faith through EE (Evangelism Explosion).

When I began to see God's potential through me, an ordinary person, I became much more excited about my Christian life. It lifted my depression as a young widow. It was exciting for me to see God at work through my ordinary abilities. One-on-one training helps the student say, "Aha, now I see it." It begins to energize their thoughts, prayers, and resources, enabling them to minister to the desperate, the neighbor, the foreigner, the brokenhearted, etc. They are filled with joy as Christ stretches their potential by faith for time, resources, and abilities.

Our Christian schools and churches often poorly prepare people for Christ's main agenda – world evangelization. Pastors usually think in terms of ministering to their congregations rather than primarily teaching their people to reach an ever-expanding world. How can we better transition from learning to practicing?

How can we go beyond our comfort zone, crossing the cultures of class, ethnic backgrounds, and lifestyles? How often do we find that even our neighbor lives in a somewhat different culture – through ethnicity, age, or income? Have you ever considered that in our neighborhoods, where there is often a Christian worker for every two hundred people, we discover many other places around the world where there is only one Christian witness for every ten thousand or every hundred thousand people? Some language groups have never received their first witness. What do we do about this huge fact?

What is amazing about Christ is that he went to another culture when he left heaven and came to this earth. He persuaded others through his relationships of love and trust.[3] He said, *As you sent me into the world, I am sending them into the world* (John 17:18 Living Bible). Well-known pastor Bill Hybels wrote a book entitled *Just Walk Across the Room*. The gist of the book is that we are called to initiate ministry.

It is exciting to consider that without limiting our next-door-neighbor responsibility, we can also respond to the heart of Jesus by investing prayers and resources globally, helping people to praise him in many languages. We can partner in sending disciple makers to places where it is difficult to live. There are people willing to learn another language and to plant the precious seeds of salvation, but they need partners. Romans 10:13-15 says: *Anyone who calls upon the name of the Lord will be saved. But how shall they ask him to save them unless they believe in him? And how can they believe in him if they have never heard about him? And how can they hear about him unless someone tells them? And how will anyone go and tell them unless someone **sends him**?* (Living Bible, emphasis added)

Andrew Murray said, *"This may be a commandment of burden bringing bondage and condemnation unless we know the twofold secret that brings the power of performance. That secret is first—the faith that love is the inward law of our new nature, and that the Spirit of God's law is within us to enable us gladly to love, and bless, and save those around us. Second, that is in the surrender to a life of close following and continual fellowship with the Lord Jesus—rejoicing in Him, forsaking all for Him, yielding all to the service of His love—that our spiritual nature can be strengthened."*

Can we not consider sending missionaries where there is no

witness, no personal soul winning? If we daily pray for the Lord to send workers as he commanded, are we not also winning? If we encourage our children in ministry opportunities and mission trips, are we not also winning people to Jesus vicariously? Often a missionary touches people who have no relatives who are Christians. Those "seeds" can produce abundant fruit when they are discipled and when they multiply. Because people prayed for me and supported me, I was able to plant the seed of the gospel in Taiwan. In many of my Bible studies, not a single new Christian had a relative that had ever known of Jesus.

Does it ever seem to you that Satan opposes ministries next door and globally? He often gives us feelings of guilt and inadequacy. Revelation 12:10-11 says: "*Now have come the salvation and the power and the kingdom of our God, and the authority of his Messiah. For the **accuser of our brothers** [and sisters], who accuses them before our God day and night, has been hurled down. They triumphed over him by the blood of the Lamb and by the word of their testimony; they did not love their lives so much as to shrink from death*" (NIV, emphasis added).

Therefore, can we step into the super blessing of uniting in his awesome plan? Watching those ordinary people – missionaries totally sold out to him – made me want to join his Great Commission. It would not be easy, but it is exciting. Under his authority and redeemed by his precious blood, we can see Satan defeated.

THE ACTION PLAN
UPWARD: A Growing Devotional and Prayer Life.

A Personal Relationship: As we model his message, it means a continual decrease of self and an increase of Christ. This happens as we spend time with Jesus in Bible study, worship, praise, and prayer. We need humility about our strengths and weaknesses, yet at the same time, we need to focus on Christ's strength, forgetting ourselves, and asking his Spirit to work beyond our abilities.[4]

A Disciplined Body: When we give Christ our best, including our body, it makes sense to eat healthy foods, exercise, and be committed to sexual purity of both body and mind.

A Spirit-Led Mind: We consider the importance of good reading, a positive mental attitude, and choosing good teacher-mentors, as a soldier prepares for spiritual battle.

Proper Priorities: Only people will live forever. Christ valued people more than even his own life. God made us for relationships with himself and others. We are to value people more than fleeting material things that cannot last.

A Simple Lifestyle: When we value people and eternal investments more than material things, we decrease pressure in our lives. We can be content. A simple lifestyle frees us to invest in eternity. The apostle Paul encouraged Christians to give generously, not because God has a need, but because of the eternal rewards they would receive in doing so. Stanley Tam of US Plastics, Lima, Ohio, put himself on a limited salary and turned over the profits of his business to help plant churches. His reward increased. Now he supports more than 100 church-planting teams in areas of the world where they have never heard of Jesus. In Randy Alcorn's book *The Treasure Principle*, he says, "God prospers me not to raise my standard of living but to raise my standard of giving."[6]

A Concentration on the Most Important Values: Disciple makers never stop learning. They stay connected to the learner. They focus on the vision of Christ and his agenda. They never stop praying, encouraging, loving, and caring. Disciple makers are multiplying witnesses by doing these things.

A GROWING MINISTRY THROUGH GODLY FRIENDSHIP

Connect: Christ reached out to the masses in the marketplaces, on the hillsides, and in people's homes. He had compassion. He fed people, healed the sick, and gave wonderful words of hope. However, he knew people often followed him for the wrong reasons.

Select: Look for **FAT** (Faithful, Available, Teachable) people. Our children are the best place to begin. Christ selected the twelve. He chose men who were available, who were willing to follow and learn. We should work with our same sex.[7]

Stay Close: Associate through activities, ministries, small groups, phone calls, visits, prayer partners, etc. Be committed to your friends.[8]

Train: By listening, teaching, and example. Plan ministries together.[9]

Delegate Responsibilities: Christ asked the disciples to baptize others, handle the finances, and pass out the food. He sent them out to preach. He said they would do greater things than he did. We need to empower those showing potential with roles in ministry. We need to believe in Christ's ability to work in and through their lives. Christ sent out the seventy before they felt they were ready. They returned rejoicing.[10]

Supervise and Do Feedback: When the disciples failed to cast out a demon, they asked Jesus, "Why?" (Matthew 17:19-21 Living Bible). *"Because of your little faith,"* Jesus told them. *"For if you had faith even as small as a tiny mustard seed, you could say to this mountain, 'Move!' and it would go far away. Nothing would be impossible. But this kind of demon won't leave* unless *you have prayed and gone without food."* Jesus stays close and he is praying for us still.[11]

Focus on Reproduction: If we take those steps, so beautifully modeled by Christ as he trained the twelve, then we can multiply disciple makers. We can enjoy the fruit of their lives because we have been involved. Even as we grow older, we have a great sense of fulfillment. I'm thrilled with my Chinese friends who are now spreading the gospel. Have **fun:** When we pray together, play together, eat together, and enjoy fellowship, God molds us into an effective team. Often we help our workers face problems, and they in turn help us.

Learn to Embrace the Cross: The reason discipleship is so important is that many fall away from Christ when the going gets tough. Sometimes there are broken relationships, discouragements, illnesses, or financial crises in our lives or the lives of our godly friends. Satan wants to capture God's inheritance and silence our voice of praise. It is through these godly friendships that we can pray to bind Satan, and to be involved in bringing healing and encouragement. This affects not only our lives but also the lives of our friends and the lives of the missionaries for whom we are praying. Our missionaries are often in a fierce battle, living in a land that has long been stolen **by Satan.**

CONCLUSION

When we pray that the Lord of the harvest will send out workers (including us) into his harvest, if we think globally, that harvest also includes our next-door neighbor. However, if we consider only our neighborhood as our responsibility, then those we disciple whom the Lord wants in his **global** harvest field may have "ingrown eyeballs," and be unable to see beyond their own culture and locality.

(Endnotes)

1   Sherwood G. Ligenfelter and Marvin K. Mayers, *Ministering Cross-Culturally* (Grand Rapids, MI: Baker Book House, 1986), pp. 15-17.

2   Robert Coleman, *The Master Plan of Discipleship* (New Jersey: Revell, 1987), 8l.

3   Paul G. Hiebert, *Anthropological Insights for Missionaries* (Grand Rapids, MI: Baker Book House, 1978), 255.

4   Robert Coleman, *The Master Plan of Discipleship* (New Jersey: Revell, 1987), pp. 99-139.

5   Randy Alcorn, *The Treasure Principle* (Colorado Springs, CO: Multnomah Publishers, 2001), 75.

6   Robert Coleman, *The Master Plan of Discipleship* (New Jersey: Revell, 1987), pp. 53-55.

7   Ibid., pp. 70-76.

8   Ibid., pp. 98-119.

9   Ibid., pp. 80-85.

10 Ibid., pp. 110-118.

About the Author

V aletta first lost her son, then her husband, and finally her remaining two children. On top of that, she suffered criminal attack and rape. But not defeated, she sensed the presence of God through it all, giving her *peace that passeth understanding*. Valetta later remarried, finished college, served on a missionary training team, and has inspired thousands with her story of how the love of Jesus overcomes darkness.

Young Men of the Cross is the story of One Mission Society's commitment to do something never before attempted—to place the Gospel message in every home in a nation. Their target was Japan, which at the time had 10.4 million homes. The Great Village Campaign was launched in 1913 with young Japanese evangelists carrying Scriptures to thousands of homes on small islands, in dense forests, and across barely accessible mountain ranges. In 1917, ten young men from God's Bible School in Cincinnati volunteered to work with the Japanese evangelists to complete this monumental task.

The Second Crusade, a sequel to *Young Men of the Cross*, tells of One Mission Society's post-World War II attempt to again reach every home in Japan with the gospel. This time, the program was called the Every Creature Crusade (ECC, now known as Every Community for Christ), and young college students joined national coworkers in spreading the gospel in Japan. Later, crusaders were sent to Korea, Taiwan, and Hong Kong to take the ECC program to those OMS fields as well. One OMS leader said of the effect of the ECC in his life: "As our crusade team moved from town to town and witnessed the salvation of hundreds and the planting of scores of churches, it was this more than anything else that drew many of us back to those fields as career missionaries."

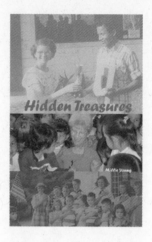

Missionary life is not what most people expect. One Mission Society missionary Millie Young shares in her biography, *Hidden Treasures*, that it is so much more than just preaching. Making daily contact, organizing camps, running Christian schools, and living among the people are vital components of ministry. It is letting the local people see you living your life, overcoming obstacles, and laughing. Millie experienced hardship and provision, joy and heartbreaking sadness, insurmountable obstacles and immense success in spreading the salvation message to the lost—especially in the rural areas of Colombia. Her missionary work is the living legacy of changed lives.

ÔNE MISSION
OMS · ONE MISSION SOCIETY

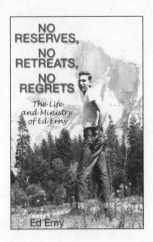

NO
RESERVES,
NO
RETREATS,
NO
REGRETS

*The Life
and Ministry
of Ed Erny*

Ed Erny

My life story begins with a preacher who, by the leading of the Spirit, refused to end a service until my father, a successful businessman, had given his heart to the Lord. I eventually followed in my father's footsteps into full-time ministry, but only after overcoming self-doubt and self-consciousness in my ability to share the gospel.

God took that doubt away when a young man gave his heart to the Lord after I told him about Jesus. From that moment on, in Taiwan, the Philippines, and other places where I served, I saw the tremendous hand of the Lord at work as I allowed Him to lead and work through me. My desire is that you will be inspired and motivated to serve the Lord as freely and willingly as I was privileged to do for many years. May you, by God's grace, determine to live with no reserves, no retreats, and no regrets.

ONEMISSION
OMS · ONE MISSION SOCIETY

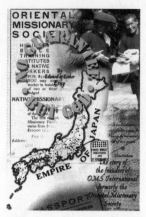

Benjamin Franklin once wrote that the two certainties of life are death and taxes. But for the Christian, certainty is so much more. *Faith is confidence in what hope for and assurance about what we do not see"* (Hebrews 11:1). By faith, with *No Guarantee but God*, Charles Cowman, Ernest Kilbourne, and Juji Nakada embarked on an adventure with God that began a missionary organization in Japan in 1901 that today spans the globe.

After graduating from Asbury College and Asbury Theological Seminary in Wilmore, Kentucky, Elmer Kilbourne and his wife Ella Ruth sailed for China. Within a year, they were forced to flee from the armies of Mao Zedong. They relocated in Korea, and the next year, in 1950, they were again forced to flee the Communist armies flooding down from the North. Elmer's heroic efforts on behalf of millions of Korean War victims are one of the greatest missionary sagas of the twentieth century.